Student Manual

of Classroom Exercises and Study Guide for

Understanding Generalist Practice

SECOND EDITION

Karen K. Kirst-Ashman
Grafton H. Hull, Jr.
Vicki Vogel

Nelson-Hall Publishers / Chicago

Printed in U.S.A.
ISBN 0-8304-1504-7

Student Workbook
to Accompany
Understanding Generalist Practice
Second Edition

Introduction

Provision of a vital study aid, on the one hand, and interesting practice applications, on the other, are the two major goals of this workbook. Each chapter has two basic sections. The first outlines the text's content for you. The intent is to help you organize the material so it's easier to remember. Major points can easily be distinguished from more minor details.

Some students use the workbook outlines to take notes as they read the text. Other students use the outlines to follow their instructors' lectures. Using the outlines can help you avoid or at least decrease "speed note taking."

This workbook's second major goal is to provide exercises and role plays to help you practice and apply the content discussed in the text. The exercises coincide with the specific practice skills explored. They are intended to make the text's material come alive for you and give you practical insights into what generalist practice is really like.

Printed in U.S.A.

Contents

1 Introducing Generalist Practice: The Generalist Intervention Model

I. Introducing Generalist Practice

A. Three Dimensions of Definition

1. Multiple level interventions
2. Knowledge base carefully chosen from a range of theories
3. Focus on private issues and social justice concerns

II. The Uniqueness of Social Work

A. Purpose of Social Work

1. Enhance the problem solving and coping capacities of people
2. Link people with systems that provide them with resources, services, and opportunities
3. Promote the effective and humane operation of these systems
4. Contribute to the development and improvement of social policy

B. Common Core of Helping Professions: Interviewing and Counseling Skills

Figure 1.1: Social Work and Other Helping Professions

C. Four Dimensions of Social Work

1. Focus attention on any problem or cluster of problems
2. Focus on targeting the environment for change
3. Advocate for client
4. Emphasis and adherence to core of professional values

III. Defining Generalist Practice

A. The Application of an Eclectic Knowledge Base, Professional Values, and a Wide Range of Skills to Target Systems of Any Size, for Change Within the Context of Four Primary Processes

1. Work effectively within an organizational structure under supervision
2. Assume wide range of professional roles
3. Apply critical thinking skills to the planned change process
4. Emphasize client empowerment

Highlight 1.1: An Outline of Concepts Involved in the Definition of Generalist Practice

Figure 1.2: The Definition of Generalist Practice: A Pictorial View

B. Defining Generalist Practice: An Eclectic Knowledge Base

1. Fields of practice
    a. Services available
2. Systems theory
    a. Focus on the interactions of various systems in the environment
        1) Individuals
        2) Groups
        3) Families
        4) Organizations
    b. Concepts of systems model

1) System: A set of elements that forms an orderly, interrelated, and functional whole

2) Dynamic: Constant movement because problems and issues are forever changing

3) Interact: Systems constantly interact with each other

4) Input: Energy, information, or communication flow received from other systems

5) Output: Energy, information, or communication flow emitted from a system

6) Homeostasis: Tendency of a system to maintain a stable, constant state of equilibrium or balance

7) Equifinality: Many different means to the same end

c. Conceptualizing workers and clients as systems

1) Client system: Individual, family, group, organization, or community that will benefit from generalist social work intervention

2) Change agent system: Individual who initiates the planned change process

3) Action system: People who agree and are committed to work together to attain proposed change

3. Ecological perspective

   a. Concept of social environment is grounded in ecological perspective

   b. Similarities between systems theory and ecological perspective

      1) Emphasize systems and focus on the dynamic interaction among levels of system

      2) Some terms and concepts are the same

      3) Each provides framework to view the world

      4) Both emphasize external interactions instead of internal functioning

   c. Differences between system theory and the ecological perspective

      1) Ecological approach refers to living, dynamic interactions and emphasis on active participation

      2) Systems theory is broader, can refer to inanimate, mechanical operation and functioning of a human family

      3) Ecological perspectives theories focus on transactions between individual and the environment at the point where the individual and environment meet

4) Systems theory addresses boundaries of subsystems within a system and maintenance of homeostasis or equilibrium within a system

d. Ecological model is more limited in scope and application than systems theory

e. Ecological concepts

1) Social environment: Conditions, circumstances, and human interactions that encompass human beings

2) Person-in-environment: People constantly interact with various systems around them

3) Transactions: Communication and interaction with others in their environment

4) Energy: Natural power of active involvement among people and their environments

5) Interface: Exact point at which the interaction between an individual and the environment takes place

6) Adaptation: Capacity to adjust to surrounding environmental conditions

7) Coping: Human adaptation and struggle to overcome problems

8) Interdependence: Mutual reliance of each person on each other person

f. Which perspective is best?

4. Curriculum content areas

a. Human behavior and the social environment

b. Social policy

1) Rules

2) Some are unfair or oppressive

c. Practice and practice skills

1) The *doing* of social work

2) Eclectic

d. Research

1) Reasons for importance

a) Help social workers be more effective in their practice and get better and clearer results

b) Helps build a foundation for planning effective interventions

c) Provides situation-specific data to inform action

2) Categories

a) Behaviors of individual clients and their interactions with others close to them

b) How services are provided to clients and how successfully they accomplish their goals

c) Social workers' attitudes and educational backgrounds

d) Study of organizations, communities, and social policy

5. Human diversity

a. Discrimination: Prejudgment and negative treatment of people based on identifiable characteristics such as race, gender, religion, or ethnicity

b. Oppression: Putting extreme limitations and constraints on some group or institution

c. Stereotypes: Fixed mental pictures of members of some specified group based on some attribute that portrays an overly simplified opinion without consideration and appreciation of individual differences

6. Promotion of social and economic justice

a. Social justice: Idea that in a perfect world all citizens would have identical rights, protection, opportunities, obligations, and social benefits

b. Economic justice: Distribution of resources in a fair and equitable manner

7. Populations-at-risk

    a. People of color

    b. Women

    c. Gay and lesbian persons

    d. Elderly

    e. Ethnic groups

    f. Difference in culture, class, or religion

    g. People with physical or mental disabilities

8. Field practicum

    a. Engages the student in supervised social work practice and provides opportunities to apply classroom learning in the field setting

9. Social work values and ethics

    a. Values: What you do and do not consider important and to have worth

    b. Ethics: Principles that specify what is good and bad, and what should and should not be done

    c. Code of Ethics—Responsibilities:

        1) To clients

        2) To colleagues

        3) In practice settings

        4) As professionals

        5) To the profession

6) To the broader society

d. Ethical dilemmas

Highlight 1.2: Ethical Dilemmas

E. Defining Generalist Practice: Application to a Wide Range of Skills to Target Systems of Any Size

1. Common generalist skills

a. Prepare

b. Communicate

c. Analyze

d. Contract

e. Roles

f. Stabilizing

2. Micro skills for generalist practice

3. Mezzo skills for generalist practice

4. Macro skills for generalist practice

F. Defining Generalist Practice: Working in an Organizational Structure Under Supervision

Highlight 1.3: The Macro Level Approach

G. Defining Generalist Practice: A Wide Range of Roles

1. Counselor: Provides guidance to clients and assists them in a planned change or problem solving process

2. Educator: Gives information and teaches skills to other systems

3. Broker: Links client systems to needed resources

4. Case manager: Coordinates, on behalf of a specific client, needed services provided by agencies, organizations, or facilities
5. Mobilizer: Identifies and convenes community people and resources to identify unmet community needs and effect changes in community
6. Mediator: Resolves arguments or disagreements among micro, mezzo, or macro systems in conflict
7. Facilitator: Guides a group experience
8. Advocate: Speaks out on behalf of clients to promote fair treatment or gain needed resources

H. Defining Generalist Practice: Critical Thinking Skills

1. Critical thinking: Ability to carefully evaluate the validity of an assumption or a so-called "fact"
2. Dimensions of critical thinking
    a. Ask questions about how clients are served and treated
    b. Be inquisitive about how interventions are supposed to work and whether they are really effective
    c. Examine assertions made as facts by evaluating arguments on both sides of an issue
    d. Use "scientific reasoning" to analyze arguments

I. Defining Generalist Practice: Planned Change

1. Planned change: Deliberate action intended to alter a situation or interfere with an expected or usual course of events

2. Problem solving: Same as change; however, has a negative connotation

J. Defining Generalist Practice: Empowerment

1. Empowerment: Increasing, emphasizing, developing, and nurturing strengths and positive attributes

2. Saleeby's principles of strengths perspective

IV. The Generalist Intervention Model (GIM)

A. Three Features:

1. Workers acquire an eclectic knowledge base, wide range of skills to target any size system, and a professional values base

2. Core seven-step planned change process that emphasizes the assessment of client strengths

3. Generalist approach—any problem can be analyzed and addressed from multiple levels of intervention

Figure 1.3: Planned Change Steps in the Generalist Intervention Model (GIM)

Figure 1.4: Initiating Micro, Mezzo, or Macro Change During Assessment

B. Planned Change Steps in the Generalist Intervention Model

1. Engagement

a. Orient yourself to problem

b. Establish communication and relationship with others addressing problem

c. Alleviate initial client anxiety

2. Assessment

Figure 1.5: Assessment in the Generalist Intervention Model(GIM)

a. Identify your client

b. Assess the client-in-situation and identify issues

   1) Micro, mezzo, macro, diversity

c. Assessment and planning

3. Planning

Figure 1.6: Planning in the Generalist Intervention Model (GIM)

a. Seven sub-steps:

   1) Work with the client

   2) Prioritize problems

   3) Translate problems into needs

   4) Evaluate levels of intervention for each need

   5) Establish primary goals

   6) Specify objectives

   7) Formalize a contract

4. Implementation

Figure 1.7: Implementation in the Generalist Intervention Model (GIM)

5. Evaluation

a. Critical for accountability

Figure 1.8: Evaluation in the Generalist Intervention Model (GIM)

6. Termination

7. Follow-Up

V. Other Practical Generalist Skills: A Perspective on the Rest of the Text

VI. Chapter Summary

EXPERIENTIAL EXERCISES AND SIMULATIONS

Seven exercises are provided for this chapter. Exercise 1 describes a simple activity to "break the ice" and help people feel more comfortable in class. In addition to serving as another ice breaker, Exercise 2 encourages students to think about their future roles in social work practice. Exercise 3 introduces students to a variety of concepts involved in generalist practice. Exercises 4 and 5 respectively explore systems and ecological concepts. Exercise 6 explores the macro approach to generalist practice versus the micro and mezzo approaches. Finally, Exercise 7 introduces students to the concepts of social work values and ethical dilemmas in practice.

Exercise 1: Breaking the Ice

A. Brief description:
You will be asked to share some personal information about yourself with the class to begin to "break the ice" in the group.

B. Objectives:
You will be able to:
1. Reveal some personal information about yourself to others in the class.
2. Begin to demonstrate your communication skills.

C. Procedure:
1. In order to introduce yourself and share some information with others in the class, take a sheet of paper and write down the following information:
    a. Your name.
    b. One adjective which describes what you like best about yourself.
    c. One adjective which describes what you like least about yourself.
    d. Your hometown or area in the city where you live.
    e. How you feel having to talk about yourself right now.
2. One person in the class should volunteer to begin. In turn, share what you've written with the rest of the class.

Exercise 2: Where Are You Going in Social Work?

A. Brief description:
You will be asked to respond to a number of questions regarding personal and professional goals.

B. Objectives:
You will be able to:
1. Clarify your interest in the field of social work.
2. Identify some of your specific areas of interest and need.
3. Tell your instructor something about yourself, especially your specific areas of interest and need.

C. Procedure:
1. Take a sheet of paper, put your name on it, and answer the following questions (label each answer with the appropriate letter):
   a. In which areas of helping are you specifically interested (for example, adoptions, mental health, work with the elderly, alcohol and other drug abuse)? List all that you can think of. If you aren't sure or don't know as yet, say so. That's OK.
   b. Ideally, what would you like to learn from this course? Please be as specific as possible. What skills do you think you really need to learn?
   c. What are your reasons for going into social work?
   d. What practice situations do you think you might run into that scare you?
   e. What strengths do you feel you bring to the field?
   f. What weaknesses do you feel you have that might affect your work in the field?
2. Break into small groups of four to six persons. Pick *two* of your answers and share them with the others in your small group.
3. Hand your papers in to your instructor.

Exercise 3: What Do Social Workers Do?

A. Brief description:
You will be given a series of vignettes which illustrate problems commonly encountered by social workers in social service agencies. Small groups then brainstorm some of the possible intervention strategies generalist social workers might consider to solve the problems involved.

B. Objectives:
You will be able to:
1. Discuss basic types of social worker interventions at micro, mezzo, and macro levels.
2. Recognize the complexity of many of the problems encountered in generalist social work practice.
3. Recognize the importance of interpersonal skills.

4. Identify some practice areas in which you could benefit from skill development.

C. Procedure:

1. Read chapter 1 and/or listen to your instructor's lecture concerning chapter 1 prior to beginning the exercise.
2. Divide into small groups of four to six persons. Below are three vignettes. Read each one and discuss possible answers to the questions following each scenario. Select one member in each group to jot down the ideas your group proposes. This is in preparation for sharing these ideas later in a discussion involving the entire class.

Vignette #1

A fifteen-year-old can hardly make it through the morning until he can meet with his dealer and get some crack. He thinks briefly how it didn't used to be this bad, how he didn't used to "need" it this much. But he doesn't want to think about that for very long. It's too uncomfortable. He rationalizes that life is short and he wants to make the most of it. Besides, all of his friends use drugs, too. He's no different.

<u>Questions for small group discussion:</u>

How might a social worker approach this young man regarding his drug use?

What questions might you as a social worker ask?

How might you encourage this young man to open up to you about his problems?

What if the young man won't say anything?

What if the young man expresses hostility or anger at you?

What types of resources might be available to help him at the micro and mezzo levels?

What types of programs and services at the macro level might be available?

What types of programs and services might be developed at the macro level?

Vignette #2

Forlorn, homeless people are starving in the streets. Public funding for a community mental health program has been drastically cut back. That program had provided a halfway house where people could stay, receive counseling, and have their medication monitored. Years ago, the long-term, inpatient mental institution had been shut down. It was much too expensive. Now with the cutbacks, the community program can barely exist. People with serious mental and emotional problems have been turned away and are roaming the streets with nowhere to go.

<u>Questions for small group discussion:</u>

What services do you feel these people need at the micro, mezzo, and macro levels?

(continued)

How might you as a generalist social work practitioner go about advocating for these people? What types of social service agencies and organizations could you target for such advocacy?

What programs could be developed?

What are some ideas for possible funding sources?

Vignette #3

A family of four who have lived on their family farm for five generations is dispossessed. They had several bad years of crop failures and were unable to pay back the loans they so desperately needed to survive at the time. They are living in their '91 Chevy station wagon now. They can't find any housing they could possibly afford even while working full-time, minimum-wage jobs.

Questions for small group discussion:

What services do you feel these people need at the micro, mezzo, and macro levels?

How might you as a generalist social work practitioner go about advocating for these people? What types of social service agencies and organizations could you target for such advocacy?

What programs could be developed?

What are some ideas for possible funding sources?

3. The small groups should then come back together to discuss their ideas. The instructor will lead the discussion. Each group's selected representative should summarize the group's findings.
4. The instructor will then lead the entire class in a discussion addressing the following questions:
   a. In summary, what types of micro, mezzo, and macro interventions did the groups discuss?
   b. What was your reaction to the complexity of the problems?
   c. Did this experience help you to see social work intervention in new ways? If so, in what new ways?
   d. Where did you "get stuck"? What problems seemed exceptionally difficult to solve?
   e. What skill areas do you feel you need to develop?

Exercise 4: Understanding Systems [1]

A. Brief description:
You will be given a description of a family and its members followed by a series of situations occurring within the family. Discussion focuses on the direct application of systems concepts to this family and its situations.

B. Objectives:
You will be able to:
1. Examine the meanings of various systems theory concepts.
2. Apply these concepts to a series of concrete family life situations.

C. Procedure:
1. After reviewing the systems theory concepts presented in the text, arrange yourselves in a circle. This allows for maximum observation of the role-play activity.
2. The instructor will describe members of a family system and other people involved with the system. (As the text describes, families are systems which lie somewhere between micro and mezzo systems.) The family you'll discuss are the Abbots.[2] The basic family system is pictured below. Rectangles indicate males; round-cornered rectangles indicate females. Double-pointing arrows indicate that the couple is married. Children are depicted by a vertical line descending from the arrow to their names. Dotted lines indicate relationships between people who are not married. The ages of characters follow their names. The specific characters are as follows:

   John Abbot and **Jill Abbot** are married. They have two children, **Ashley** and **Jack**.

   Ashley is married to **Victor Newman**. They have no children.

   Jack is married to **Nikki**. Jack and Nikki have a daughter named **Victoria**.

   Victoria is in love with **Ryan**, her boyfriend.

   Nina, a friend of Ryan's, really enters the picture a little later in the exercise.

---

[1] The description, objectives, and much of the procedure and commentary for this exercise are taken from "Exercise 1: The Family System" in K. Kirst-Ashman and C. Zastrow, *Student Manual of Classroom Exercises and Study Guide for Understanding Human Behavior and the Social Environment* (Chicago: Nelson-Hall, 1990).

[2] Thanks are extended here to Ruth Kirst who provided help regarding character development.

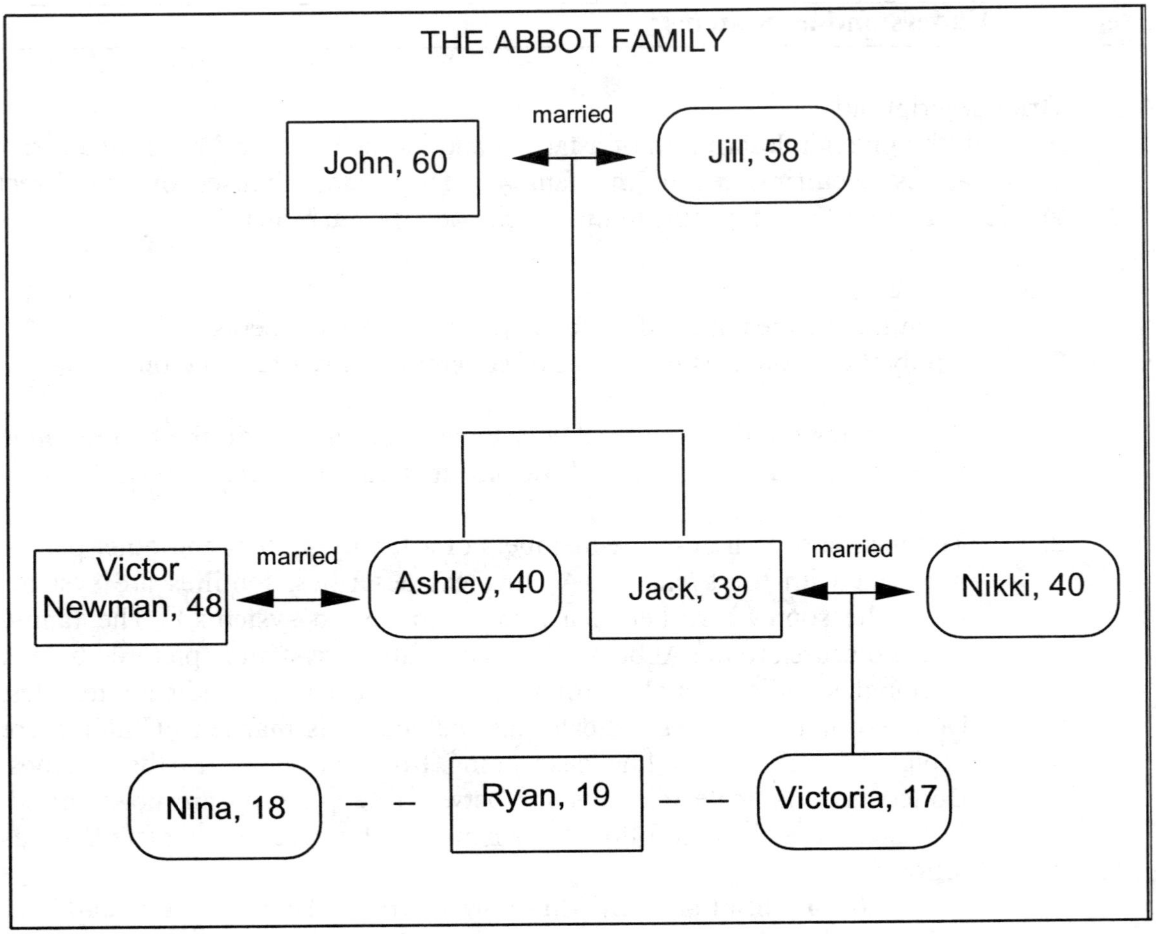

3. The instructor will ask for volunteers to play each of the characters. Each role-player's first name should be written on an eight-by-five-inch note card and placed in front of him or her so that class observers can remember who is playing what character. The family members are to sit together inside the class circle.
4. Your instructor will present the role players with a series of situations. The situations are not sequential; each stands alone. For each situation, each member involved will be asked to respond as if he or she really were that family member. Players can add any additional details they wish about the family members they play.
5. The instructor will separately present each of the following situations to the role players:

Situation #1

Jack finds out that Victor and Nikki are in love with each other. Jack is mad and moves out.

Situation #2
Victor dies of AIDS. How he contracted HIV is unknown, although Ashley suspects drug use with tainted needles. The entire family is horrified and fearful.

Situation #3
Victor is involved in the upper levels of management in DideeDry, John's paper diaper company. John owns 40 percent of the stock and is president of the company. John has a stroke and loses the use of his right side. Victor vies for control of the company. He goes to the board of directors and proposes that he take over the presidency. The board is seriously considering his request. The company needs a capable president. John is furious at Victor, as he wants to relinquish neither his control nor the presidency. John feels it will simply take some time for him to recover. Jill feels such wishful thinking is totally unrealistic.

Situation #4
Jill finds out that John had an incestuous relationship with Ashley in her early teens.

Situation #5
Victoria doubts Ryan's faithfulness and gets an HIV test. She eagerly awaits the results and tells only her mother, Nikki, about her worst fears. Much to Victoria's dismay, Nikki is so worried that she tells the rest of the family about it.

Situation #6
Ryan breaks up with Victoria. Two months later, Victoria discovers she's pregnant with Ryan's baby. Victoria runs into Ryan and Nina together. Nina announces that she and Ryan are engaged.

6. Each role player involved in the situation should share his or her feelings and describe how the situation might affect the family.
7. After receiving feedback from the individual role players, observers and role players should discuss the situation using systems theory concepts. Relate each systems theory term to the dynamics that might be occurring in the family. For example, any of the situations might upset the family's *homeostasis*. Other examples include the types of *input* and *output* involved, and the formation of various *subsystems*.

Exercise 5: Comparing Systems and Ecological Concepts

A. Brief description:
You will be given a description of a family and its members followed by a series of situations occurring within the family. Discussion focuses on the direct application of ecological concepts to this family and its situations. (This exercise

is identical to Exercise 4 above except that ecological concepts are substituted for systems theory concepts.)

B. Objectives:

You will be able to:

1. Examine the meanings of various ecological concepts.
2. Apply these concepts to a series of concrete family life situations.

C. Procedure:

1. After reviewing the ecological concepts presented in the text, arrange yourselves in a circle. This allows for maximum observation of the role-play activity.
2. Follow steps 2 through 6 presented above in Exercise 4, but replace ecological concepts with those of systems theory.

Exercise 6: Change the System, Not the Person

A. Brief description:

You will be given three vignettes and asked to propose potential solutions based on macro system (versus micro or mezzo system) changes.

B. Objectives:

You will be able to:

1. Assess problematic situations within a macro system context.
2. Propose potential macro level intervention solutions.

C. Procedure:

1. Divide up into groups of four to six persons.
2. Read the following three vignettes. Take approximately eight to ten minutes to discuss each vignette. For this exercise, do not change or move the individual. Think in terms of how the problem might be solved through macro level changes—what major organizations or community groups can do to effect change. For each vignette, focus on the following questions:

   What policies might be changed?

   What community services might be developed?

   What might your strategies be to achieve these changes and services?

   (Remember, do not change the individual. Focus only on macro system change.)

Vignette #1

You are a public social services worker in a rural county. Your job includes doing everything from helping the elderly obtain their social security payments to investigating alleged child abuse. Within the past six months, six farm families in the county have gone bankrupt. Government farm subsidies which used to be available have been withdrawn. It's been a bad past two years for crops. Now the banks are threatening to foreclose on the farm mortgages. Thus, the six families will literally be put out in the cold with no money and no place to go.

What do you do?

Vignette #2

You are a social worker for Burp County Social Services. It's a rural county with a few towns of ten thousand people but none larger. Your job as intake worker is to do family assessments when people call up with problems (anything from domestic violence to coping with serious illnesses). Your next task is to make referrals to the appropriate services.

You have been hearing about a number of sexual assaults in the area. Women are expressing fear for their safety. People who have been assaulted don't know where to turn. The nearest large cities are over eighty miles away. You have always been interested in women's issues and advocacy for women.

Now what do you do?

Vignette #3

You have a seventy-year-old client named Harriet living in an old, near-inner-city neighborhood in a large city. Since her husband died seven years ago, she's been living alone. She has no children. She is still in good health and likes to be independent.

The problem is that her house has been condemned for new highway construction. The plans are to tear it down within six months. There is no public housing available for the elderly within five miles of where she lives. She would like to stay in the area because she's got a lot of elderly friends there.

Now what? (Remember, don't move Harriet.)

Exercise 7: Resolving Ethical Dilemmas

A. Brief description:

The ethical dilemma presented involves making tough decisions about the distribution of limited resources. You will be asked to make decisions regarding who is to receive and who is not to receive urgently needed resources.

B. Objectives:

You will be able to:

1. Recognize the fact that ethical dilemmas exist which have no perfect solution.
2. Identify your personal values with respect to the situations presented.
3. Recognize the importance of ethical decision making in social work practice.

C. Procedure:

1. Make decisions on an individual basis regarding the following situation:

   You have $30,000 to spend. You must choose where it will be spent. Below are ten situations. Each situation requires spending the full amount of $30,000 in order to do any good. Dividing the money up would be useless. It would help no one.

   Which of the following persons should have the $30,000 made available to help them?

   a. A premature infant (born three months early) who must be maintained in an incubator and receive medical treatment.
   b. A fifty-two-year-old man who needs a heart transplant in order to survive.
   c. A fifty-two-year-old man who needs a heart transplant in order to survive and who also happens to be your father.
   d. A five-year-old child with AIDS.
   e. You, who have graduated but have been out of work for six months.
   f. A divorced single mother with three children, a tenth-grade education, and nothing but the clothes on her back.
   g. A person with a cognitive disability who needs to live in a group home.
   h. A fourteen-year-old runaway who is addicted to cocaine and alcohol, has been prostituting herself to survive, and needs the money to enter a drug treatment program.
   i. Rehabilitation for a convicted child sexual abuser who himself was sexually abused as a child.
   j. A dispossessed urban family consisting of a couple in their late 20s and their three small children.
2. As an individual, decide how you would choose to spend the limited resources.
3. Subsequently, participate in a discussion involving the entire class. Your instructor can help you address the following questions and issues:
   a. Who should receive priority in receiving needed funds?
   b. What criteria should be used to make such decisions?
   c. What personal values did you employ in making your decision?
   d. What issues and considerations made decision making difficult?
   e. To what extent is such a decision-making situation similar to or different from situations and decisions you have encountered in real life?
   f. What could help you make such decisions more easily?

2 Micro Practice Skills: Working with Individuals

I. Introduction

II. Micro Skills and the Generalist Intervention Model (GIM)

KNOW

Plan Change Process

A. Engagement: Establish an initial relationship with an individual or group of individuals (initial relationship)

B. Assessment: Must talk and relate to other individuals effectively to solicit enough information about the issue or problem involved to initiate positive change

C. Planning: Involves working integrally with client to establish plan of action

D. Implementation: Working with others in environment to achieve goals

E. Evaluation: Communicate with client and others to validate accomplishments

F. Follow-Up: Solicit information regarding how planned change goals have been maintained

III. Interviewing: A Key Micro Skill

IV. Beginning the Worker/Client Relationship

V. Verbal and Nonverbal Behavior

A. Eye Contact

1. Direct contact is important

2. Do not maintain continuous eye contact

3. Be aware of cultural differences where direct eye contact is considered disrespectful, insincere, or rude

B. Attentive Listing

1. Listening focuses on comprehending the meaning of what is said

a. Three aspects of communication

1) Intent

2) Impact

3) Environmental barriers

Figure 2.1: Barriers to Attentive Listening

C. Facial Expressions

D. Body Positioning

1. Tense/relaxed

2. Formal/informal

3. Zones of interaction

a. Intimate: Skin contact to eighteen inches

b. Personal: eighteen inches to four feet

c. Social: Four feet to twelve feet

1) Contact with clients should occur in the closer half of this zone

d. Public: Outward from twelve feet

e. May not be the same for all cultural backgrounds

4. Office space positioning

a. Sitting behind desk implies greater formality

VI. Warmth, Empathy, and Genuineness

A. Warmth: Conveying a feeling of interest, concern, well-being, and affection to another individual

1. Verbal

2. Nonverbal

B. Empathy: Acknowledgement that you understand the client's situation

Highlight 2.1: Practicing Empathic Responses

1. Intent

2. Impact

3. Barriers to communication

C. Genuineness: Continue to be yourself, despite the fact you are working to accomplish goals in your professional role

VII. Client Self-Determination and Empowerment

A. Self-Determination: Ethical principle in social work which recognizes the rights and needs of clients to be free to make their own choices and decisions

B. Empowerment: Process of helping individuals, families, groups, and communities to increase their strengths and develop influence toward improving their circumstances

VIII. Starting the Interview

A. The Interview Setting

B. How to Dress for the Interview and for the Job

C. Thinking Ahead about an Interview with a Client

1. Gather specific information that will be needed
2. Time frame should be clearly specified
3. Purpose of interview

D. Initial Introductions

1. Be knowledgeable about cultural differences

E. Alleviating Client's Anxiety

1. "Start where the client is"

F. Portraying Confidence and Competence

Highlight 2.2: Using Direct and Indirect Questions

G. Beginning Statement of Purpose and Role

1. Clearly explain the interview's purpose to the client
2. Explain the worker's role to the client
3. Encourage client feedback on the purpose
4. Convey to the client the usefulness of the interview

IX. Conducting the Interview

A. Verbal Responses to the Client

1. Simple encouragement
2. Rephrasing
3. Reflective responding
4. Clarification
5. Interpretation
6. Providing information
7. Empowerment: Emphasizing clients' strengths

Highlight 2.3: Stressing Client Strengths

a. Client behaviors

b. Personal qualities

c. Client's resources

8. Self-disclosure

a. Your professional role

b. Feelings and impressions about client and client's behavior

c. Perceptions concerning your ongoing interaction and relationship with client

d. Relating aspects about your own life or problems

1) Be certain it is really for the client's benefit and not your own

2) Self-disclose for some definite purpose

3) Should be short and simple

Figure 2.2: Personal versus Professional Relationships

9. Summarization

Highlight 2.4: Telling a Client What to Do

10. Eliciting information

a. Open-ended questions

b. Closed-ended questions

11. The use of *why*

12. Overlap of techniques

13. Interviewing, specific techniques, and the planned change process

X. Challenges in Interviewing

A. Dealing with Diversity: Cross-Cultural Awareness in Interviewing

1. Ongoing, continuous process

   a. Individualism is important

2. Extent to which clients are assimilated into "mainstream" culture

3. Attention to stereotypes, prejudices, discrimination, and oppression that negatively affect people from various ethnic and racial groups

4. Self-awareness of one's own ethnic and cultural background, and how it may affect a worker's ability to practice

B. Silence in the Interview

1. Client-initiated silence

   a. Gain time to organize thoughts

   b. Attempt to pressure worker to give some response or solution to a problem

   c. Resistance to or rejection of the worker's authority

2. Negative worker-initiated silence

3. Focusing on the client instead of yourself

4. Therapeutic worker-initiated silence

   a. Pacing the interview

   b. Silent focusing

   c. Responding to defenses

   d. Silent caring

C. Confronting Clients

1. Four major types of discrepancies
    a. Between two statements
    b. Between what one says and what one does
    c. Between statements and nonverbal behavior
    d. Between two or more people
2. Four components of confrontations
    a. Worker should communicate that she cares about the client and is interested in the client's well-being
    b. Worker should clearly express the client's stated goal within the problem-solving process
    c. Worker should illustrate exactly what the discrepancy is
    d. Worker should indicate the realistic results of the discrepancy
3. Suggestions for maximizing the use of confrontation
    a. Consider whether the relationship with the client is strong enough to withstand the confrontation
    b. Be aware of client's emotional state
    c. Use confrontations infrequently and only when you must
    d. Continue to demonstrate respect for client throughout the confrontation
    e. Remain empathic throughout the confrontation
    f. Use "I" statements during the confrontation
    g. Have patience and allow the client some time to change

D. Involuntary Clients

1. Acknowledge to yourself that the client is involuntary

2. Try to put yourself in your client's shoes

Highlight 2.5: Handling Hostility

3. Label and help client express negative feeling

4. Know the limits of your authority and power over the client

5. Figure out what you can do for the client that he wants

6. Cultivate hope and convey encouragement

7. Allow client time to gain trust in you and in the intervention process

8. Accept the fact that the client has the right to choose whether or not to cooperate

E. Suspicion of Untruth

1. Evaluate the situation logically

2. Examine the client's pattern of prior behavior

3. Consider not confronting the client if this is the first time the possibility of lying has come up

4. Evaluate the costs of believing or not believing your client

XI. Terminating the Interview

A. Mention how much time is left (e.g., five or fifteen minutes)

B. Tell the client how you feel as the interview is coming to a close

C. Ask clients to summarize what they have learned and accomplished

XII. Chapter Summary

Figure 2.3: Social Work Roles with Micro Systems

1. Broker: Links clients with needed resources
2. Enabler: Provides support, encouragement, and suggestions
3. Mediator: Helps conflicting parties settle disputes and agree on compromises
4. Educator: Conveys information to a client
5. Evaluator: Determines effectiveness of their own practice
6. Case manager/coordinator: Seeks out resources, plans how they might be delivered, organizes service provision, and monitors progress
7. Advocate: Champions the rights of others

EXPERIENTIAL EXERCISES AND SIMULATIONS

Nine exercises are included for this chapter. Since micro practice skills form the basis for mezzo and macro practice, these skills are especially important to master. The exercises follow chapter 2's content very closely. They are designed to apply many of the specific skills discussed.

Exercise 1 concerns increasing awareness of nonverbal behavior. Exercise 2 addresses enhancing listening ability. Exercise 3 provides opportunities to practice empathic responses. Exercise 4 features self-exploration with the intent of more clearly defining one's own genuineness. Exercise 5 involves asking direct and indirect questions. Exercise 6 allows you to practice a wide range of responses.

The final exercises deal with difficult situations frequently encountered in practice. Exercises 7, 8, and 9 address, respectively, uncomfortable silence, hostility, and suspicion of untruth within the context of practice interviews.

Exercise 1: Noting Nonverbal Behavior

A. Brief description:
Students break up into pairs. Taking turns, each describes for the other some minor problem she or he is experiencing while the other observes nonverbal behavior.

B. Objectives:
You will be able to:
1. Identify various aspects of nonverbal behavior.
2. Articulate and provide feedback about such behavior.

C. Procedure:
1. Review the material on nonverbal behavior in the text.
2. Think of and write down a brief summary of some minor problem currently being experienced. Since you will be asked to share it, it should be something that is not too personal. For example, it might be how someone you live with doesn't pick up his or her dirty socks or insists that you do the dishes immediately after eating. It can be any small thing that annoys you.
3. Break up into pairs. In the event that there is an odd number in class, form one group of three.
4. Members in each pair take turns being the talker and the observer. The talker should briefly explain to the observer the problem he or she previously wrote down. This should take approximately five minutes. The observer may ask questions of the talker for clarification. However, the talker should do the majority of the talking.
5. While the talker is talking, the observer should write down brief notes concerning the talker's nonverbal behavior in the following three areas (for each area, a number of questions are raised to indicate some specific aspects of behavior the observer can note):

Eye Contact

To what extent does the talker look you in the eye while explaining his or her problem?

Does the talker appear to be comfortable in making eye contact with you, or does he or she frequently look away in a nervous gesture?

Might there be some cultural differences between you and the talker that would affect the extent to which eye contact is appropriate?

Facial Expressions

How would you describe the talker's facial expressions as she or he describes the problem?

What specific facial movements indicate concern, humor, anger, embarrassment, or other emotions? (*continued*)

What specific facial movements seem to emphasize the points that the talker appears to feel are the most significant?

Body Positioning

What specific aspects of the talker's body positioning indicate that she or he is tense or relaxed or somewhere in between?

What specific aspects of the talker's body positioning indicate either a formal or informal style in presenting information?

How tense/relaxed and formal/informal do you feel yourself as you sit there observing the talker?

What zone of personal space exists between you and the talker?

To what extent is this zone comfortable or uncomfortable to you under these conditions?

6. After approximately five minutes of listening to the talker, the observer should take a few minutes to note whatever information she or he can remember about the talker's nonverbal behavior but didn't have a chance to record earlier. These notes can be rough and brief as they will only be used by the observer to give the talker feedback.
7. The observer should now provide feedback to the talker concerning his or her nonverbal behavior. The observer should use the notes recorded during the activity's process. This should take about five minutes.
8. Each pair should now reverse the roles of talker and observer. They should follow procedural steps 4 through 7, except that their roles are reversed. (In the event that there is one group of three, one of the three will be an observer twice instead of assuming a talking role.)
9. After all feedback concerning nonverbal behavior has been given, the entire class should discuss the experience together. The instructor will focus on the following questions, among others:
    a. What types of nonverbal behaviors in the four areas did you notice?
    b. What aspects of nonverbal behavior, if any, did this exercise help to sensitize you to?
    c. How did participating in this exercise feel?
    d. What did you learn from this exercise?

Exercise 2: "Listen Up"

A. Brief description:
The class will break up into pairs. Each person takes turns speaking about an issue or listening to what the other says. They then compare the *intent* of the talker with the communication's *impact* upon the listener.

B. Objectives:
You will be able to:
1. Examine your ability to listen accurately.
2. Compare the intent of a sender's messages with the impact upon yourself as listener.

C. Procedure:
1. Take a moment to focus on some problem you have or some issue about which you have exceptionally strong feelings (for instance, a political issue or a religious stance). It's important that you select a topic about which you have strong feelings and opinions.
2. Divide into pairs.
3. Take turns at being talker and listener. The first talker (Talker #1) should spend three minutes describing the problem or issue "off the top of his or her head." The listener (Listener #1) should remain completely silent. No written notes should be taken. It's important to rely on memory alone when it's time to give feedback.
4. Your instructor will alert you when the three minutes are up. At that point, talkers should remain silent while listeners relate to talkers what they heard talkers say. The instructor will allot three minutes for this.
5. At the end of this three-minute period, the talker and listener should answer the following questions. Do so silently without letting each other know what you're writing.

Questions for the Talker:

a. To what extent did you feel the listener heard the major *intent* of what you were trying to say? (Circle a number.)

Didn't listen to me at all				Listened to me moderately well				Listened to me extremely well	
1	2	3	4	5	6	7	8	9	10

b. To what extent do you feel that the listener heard what you had to say *with accurate detail*? (Circle a number.)

Little or no accurate detail				Moderately accurate detail				Extremely accurate detail	
1	2	3	4	5	6	7	8	9	10

c. *What percentage of all that you said* did the listener relate back to you? ________ %

d. What were the *major errors and inaccuracies* evident in the listener's feedback? ______________________________

____

Questions for the Listener:

a. To what extent did you feel you heard the major *intent* of what the talker was trying to say? (Circle a number.)

Not at all				Moderately well				Extremely well	
1	2	3	4	5	6	7	8	9	10

b. To what extent do you feel that you heard what the talker had to say *with accurate detail*? (Circle a number.)

Little or no accurate detail				Moderately accurate detail				Extremely accurate detail	
1	2	3	4	5	6	7	8	9	10

c. *What percentage of all that the talker said* did you relate back to him or her? ________ %

d. What specific topics and areas did you *not understand or remember* very well? ______________________________

____

____

____

6. Now exchange roles and repeat steps 3 through 5. Because your roles are reversed, it's appropriate for you to complete the alternate talker/listener questionnaire. Once again, do so silently without showing each other what you've written.

7. In each pair, you can now share with each other your results. Remember that the Talker Questionnaire for one should be contrasted with the Listener Questionnaire for the other. Between the two of you, take five to ten minutes to discuss the following questions and issues:

   a. To what extent did you agree in each experience that the talker's intent (that is, what the talker intended to say) coincided with the listener's impact (that is, what the listener heard)?
   b. To what extent did you agree in each experience on the amount of detail that the listener actually heard?

c. For each experience, how did your percentages compare regarding how much of what the talker said was related back by the listener?

d. For each experience, compare and contrast the talker's perception of the listener's feedback with the listener's inability to understand or remember what the talker said.

8. The instructor will recall the pairs for a general class discussion. Address the following questions:

a. What differences did you find between what talkers said and what listeners heard?

b. What types of information were omitted in the listeners' feedback?

c. What thoughts and ideas did you gain from this exercise about communication and attentive listening?

Exercise 3: Practicing Empathic Responses

A. Brief description:
You will be asked to demonstrate empathic responses to a variety of case vignettes.

B. Objectives:
You will be able to:
1. Identify various ways you can verbally demonstrate empathy.
2. Apply empathic phrases to simulated case situations.

C. Procedure:
1. Review the section on warmth and empathy discussed in the text.
2. The instructor will read the series of case situations illustrated below, and will then ask for a volunteer to respond with an empathic response.
3. The following are some examples of leading phrases which you can use to begin an empathic statement:
   - My impression is that . . .
   - It appears to me that . . .
   - Is what you're saying that . . . ?
   - Do I understand you correctly that . . . ?
   - I'm hearing you say that . . .
   - Do you mean that . . . ?
   - Do you feel that . . . ?
   - I feel that you . . .
   - I'm getting the message that . . .
   - You seem to be . . .
   - When you say that, I think you . . .
   - You look as if you . . .
   - You sound so ________. Can we talk more about it?
   - You look ___________. What's been happening?

4. Your instructor will read and ask you to respond to the five case vignettes cited below. After each case, the class can discuss the following two questions:
   a. What various responses are possible in this case situation?
   b. How do various responses compare and contrast in terms of their effectiveness?

Vignette #1

You are a social worker in foster care. You're making a home visit to one of the foster homes on your caseload. The purpose is to talk with both foster parents and determine how things are going with their nine-year-old foster child, Katie. The couple have three children of their own, all of whom are in college. In the past the foster couple has expressed some interest in adopting Katie. When you get to the home, only the mother is present. After polite initial greetings, the foster mother states, "Katie certainly doesn't like to read very much like the rest of us. I think she gets bored when she's not doing something active. Many times I just don't know what to do with her."

You *empathically* respond . . . (Remember that you *do not* have to solve the problem right now. You only need to let your client know that you understand how she feels.)

Vignette #2

You are a social worker in a health care facility for the elderly. Helen is a resident who has been living there for approximately two years. All rooms have two residents, which has consistently been a problem for Helen. Her current roommate is Hilda, a quiet woman who rarely interacts with any of the other residents. Helen is very possessive of her things and wants no one else to touch them. Additionally, Helen does not like to share the bathroom, which is also used by the two residents in the next room. Helen, a strong, outspoken woman even at age ninety-seven, approaches you and states, "Hilda keeps using my bathroom and pushes my things around. I want her out of there right now! You do something right now!"

You *empathically* respond . . .

Vignette # 3

You are a school social worker. Romy, age sixteen, was in the men's bathroom when several other students were caught using drugs. Romy insists it was the others who were guilty and he was innocent. He said he just happened to be in the restroom at the same time. The teacher who found them couldn't distinguish who was guilty and who was not, so put them all on "penalty." That means detentions after school and exclusion from any sports for two weeks. Romy is furious. He comes up to you and states, "It's not fair! It's just not fair! I'm innocent and I'm getting punished anyway. I should've used the drugs if I'm going to get the punishment."

You *empathically* respond . . .

Vignette # 4

You are a social worker at a diagnostic and treatment center for children who have multiple disabilities. Your primary function is to work with parents, helping them to cope with the pressures they are under and connecting them with resources they need. A mother of a five-year-old boy with severe cerebral palsy[1] talks with you on a weekly basis. Her son is very disabled. He has very little muscular control. He can't walk by himself or talk, although his speech, occupational, and physical therapists feel he has normal intelligence. The mother's husband is of a religion that denies the existence of disease and of physical impairment. Thus, he denies that his son has a disability. The burden of caretaking rests solely upon the mother. She loves her son dearly and generally does what she can for him enthusiastically. She enters your office one day, says hello, and sits down. She immediately puts her hand to her eyes and breaks down in tears.

You *empathically* respond . . .

---

[1] *Cerebral palsy* is a condition of the brain that results from damage before or during birth. Symptoms include difficulties in speech and mobility.

Exercise 4: What Is Your Own Brand of Genuineness?

A. Brief description:
Students are asked to respond to a questionnaire about their individual personality traits.

B. Objectives:
You will be able to:
1. Identify some of your own individual personality traits.
2. Explore how these traits might affect your relationships in social work practice.

C. Procedure:
1. Complete the following *Who Are You?* questionnaire as honestly as possible. You do not need to share your answers unless you choose to. Take approximately ten to fifteen minutes to complete the questionnaire.

Who Are You?
(A Self-Exploratory Questionnaire)

1) Complete the following four *who are you* statements. They can be adjectives, nouns, or longer statements. If you had to summarize who you are, what would you say?
I am ______________________________
I am ______________________________
I am ______________________________
I am ______________________________

2) What adjectives would you use to describe yourself? Circle all that apply. They are in no particular order or priority. They are just meant to stimulate your thinking about yourself.

Happy Sad Honest Dishonest Sensitive Insensitive
Trustworthy Untrustworthy Caring Uncaring Outgoing
Shy Withdrawn Friendly Unfriendly Religious
Not very religious Nervous Calm Formal Informal
Aggressive Assertive Timid Confident Careful Careless
Not very confident Capable Incapable Independent Dependent
Affectionate Cool Wary Bold Cheerful Witty
Unassuming Thorough Easy-going Determined Clever
Responsive Strong-minded Weak-willed (at least sometimes)
Leisurely Industrious Controlled Spontaneous Serious
Funny Tough Pleasant Daring Eager Efficient
Not so efficient Artistic Tactful Intolerant Vulnerable
Likable Smart Understanding Impatient Patient
(continued)

Imaginative Wordy Concise Open-minded Funny
Organized Somewhat disorganized Conscientious Late
Emotional Unemotional Open Creative Curious Sincere
Precise A little haphazard Cooperative Ethical Brave
Mature Eager Spunky

3) Cite your four greatest strengths. They can involve anything from personal qualities to talents to accomplishments. They don't have to be in any particular order or priority.
Strength A ______________________________________
Strength B ______________________________________
Strength C ______________________________________
Strength D ______________________________________

4) Cite your four greatest weaknesses. These don't have to be in any order or priority either.
Weakness A ______________________________________
Weakness B ______________________________________
Weakness C ______________________________________
Weakness D ______________________________________

5) How do you think your personal strengths will help you to work with clients in social work practice?
____
____
____
____

6) What weaknesses, if any, do you think you need to work on to improve your ability to work with clients in social work practice?
____
____
____
____
____

2. After you've had time to complete the questionnaire, your instructor will lead a class discussion by asking you the following questions:
   a. In general, what types of personal qualities do you think are helpful when working with clients in social work practice?
   b. What personal strengths do you have that you think will be useful in the field?

Exercise 5: Asking Direct and Indirect Questions

A. Brief description:
You will be asked to phrase both direct and indirect questions in response to a variety of situations.

B. Objectives:
You will be able to:
1. Recognize the difference between direct and indirect questions.
2. Respond with such questions to simulated case situations.

C. Procedure:
1. Review the material in the text on using direct and indirect questions. Generally, direct questions are those that clearly ask for information. They usually can be identified because they end in a question mark. Indirect questions, on the other hand, ask questions more subtly. They imply a leading question, usually hidden in some direct statement.
2. In a class discussion, the instructor will ask for volunteers to respond to various needs for information. First you will be asked how you might phrase a direct question in order to get the information you need. Then, you will be asked how to do so using an indirect question. After each answer, the class will discuss the question's strengths and weaknesses.
3. Consider the needs for information presented below. How might you phrase (1) a *direct* question, and how might you phrase (2) an *indirect* question to obtain the information? Supply these two questions for each of the following situations.
   a. What a single fifteen-year-old who is six months pregnant plans to do about her baby.
   b. What a single, eighty-nine-year-old woman, still living in her own home but experiencing rapidly failing health, plans to do about her future.
   c. How a recently divorced single mother plans to care for her three small children when she returns to work.
   d. What a twenty-three-year-old man just out of prison and on probation (he had been convicted on several burglary charges) plans to do to support himself.
   e. How much a thirty-five-year-old man convicted of drunk driving drinks.
   f. What the financial resources are of a couple in their thirties applying to adopt a baby.
   g. How a twelve-year-old girl with a cognitive disability (who has been designated as "mildly retarded") feels about her new special education teacher.
   h. How many friends a shy, eight-year-old boy has in his neighborhood.
   i. The amount of stress a fifty-three-year-old female executive is experiencing in her high-level administrative position.

j. How well a couple in their twenties who claim they're experiencing marital difficulties are able to communicate with each other.

4. Now, discuss the following questions:
   a. How difficult was it to think up the questions, especially the indirect ones?
   b. How would you describe indirect questions, using your own words?
   c. What are the strengths and weaknesses of using direct and indirect questions?
   d. In what ways are indirect questions able to get at the needed information?
   e. What did you learn from participating in this exercise?

Exercise 6: How to Respond to Clients

A. Brief description:
You will be asked to respond to a variety of simulated client statements using a range of response types.

B. Objectives:
You will be able to:
1. Identify a variety of response types.
2. Recognize and explain differences among the types of responses.
3. Propose a variety of responses to simulated client situations.

C. Procedure:
1. Review information in the text concerning interviews, especially focusing on verbal responses to clients. Make certain you understand how each type of response is defined and how they differ.
2. Break down into small groups of four to six persons.
3. Below are a number of statements typically made by clients. For each statement, work with your other group members to propose and write down examples of the different types of responses possible. Here is an example:

   <u>Example of client statement:</u> **"I'm so disgusted with my life!"**
   Possible responses:
   Simple encouragement: "Mm-mm, please go on."
   Rephrasing: "You're fed up with what's happening."
   Reflective responding: "It seems that you are upset."
   Clarification: "Do you mean that you don't like what's happening in your personal relationships?"
   Interpretation: "Perhaps things are overwhelming you so that you feel trapped."

Providing information: "I can refer you to someone who can talk to you about your problems and, hopefully, help you resolve them."

Emphasizing clients' strengths: "It's good that you're getting in touch with your feelings and have chosen to share them with me. That's usually the first step in working problems out."

Self-disclosure: "Sometimes, I feel pretty disgusted, too."

Summarization (granted, it is pretty hard to summarize one measly line, so feel free to make up a summary): "So far we've discussed a number of your problems, including finances and relationships. You've also indicated how disgusted you are at this point."

Eliciting information—Closed question: "Have you just started to feel this way?"

Eliciting information—Open-ended question: "What are your reasons for being so disgusted?"

Client Statement #1: "I'm really worried about my mother."

Possible Responses:

Simple encouragement: ______________________________

____

____

Rephrasing: ______________________________

____

____

Reflective responding: ______________________________

____

____

Clarification: ______________________________

____

____

Interpretation: ______________________________

____

____

Providing information: ______________________________

____

____

Emphasizing clients' strengths: ______________________________

____

____

Self-disclosure: ______________________________

____

____

Summarization: ______________________________

____

____

Eliciting information—closed question: ______________________________
____
____

Eliciting information—open-ended question: __________________________
____
____

Client Statement #2: "Hell's bells! I've got so much work to do that I don't know where to start."

Possible responses:

Simple encouragement: ____
____
____

Rephrasing: ____
____
____

Reflective responding: ____
____
____

Clarification: ____
____
____

Interpretation: ____
____
____

Providing information: ____
____
____

Emphasizing clients' strengths: ______________________________________
____
____

Self-disclosure: ____
____
____

Summarization: ____
____
____

Eliciting information—closed question: ______________________________
____
____

Eliciting information—open-ended question: __________________________
____
____

Client Statement #3: "My dad beat me up last night."
Possible responses:

Simple encouragement: ______________________________

Rephrasing: ______________________________

Reflective responding: ______________________________

Clarification: ______________________________

Interpretation: ______________________________

Providing information: ______________________________

Emphasizing clients' strengths: ______________________________

Self-disclosure: ______________________________

Summarization: ______________________________

Eliciting information—closed question: ______________________________

Eliciting information—open-ended question: ______________________________

Client Statement #4: "My little girl Grizelda is three-and-a-half, and hasn't started to walk yet."
Possible responses:

Simple encouragement: ______________________________

Rephrasing: ______________________________

Reflective responding: ______________________________

Clarification: ______________________________

Interpretation: ______________________________

Providing information: ______________________________

Emphasizing clients' strengths: ______________________________

Self-disclosure: ______________________________

Summarization: ______________________________

Eliciting information—closed question: ______________________________

Eliciting information—open-ended question: ______________________________

Client Statement #5: "I just don't have enough money to pay the rent. What should I do?"

Possible responses:

Simple encouragement: That must feel very overwhelming -

Rephrasing: So your having a hard time with your finances

Reflective responding: It seems that you are asking for help - (Feeling word)

you don't have enough income to make your monthly rent —

Clarification: Do you mean you do not have any or enough money for your rent

Interpretation: your frustrated with your income and need some assistance.

Providing information: I can refer you to an agency who can talk to you about your situation & offer some helpful hints

Emphasizing clients' strengths: Its good that you were able to admit / recognize your problem and ask / seek help –

Self-disclosure: sometimes I feel I need to seek help as well

Summarization: We have just discussed the problem of not enough income and a referal, You have acknowledged that you are frustrated as well –

Eliciting information—closed question: ~~What do you~~ How long ~~has the problem been an issue~~ have you had this feeling of frustration?

Eliciting information—open-ended question: What do you think are some possible resolutions to your problem — ? pg. 43

4. After about thirty minutes, your instructor will ask the small groups to join together in a class discussion. Address the following questions:
   a. Which types of response statements did you feel were the most difficult to develop?
   b. Which types of response statements were the easiest to think up?
   c. For each client statement, which types of response statements seem to fit best? For what reasons?
   d. To what extent did you feel that there was overlap among response types? Please specify exactly where you felt there was such overlap.

Group names - Rob, Karyn, & Bertha

Exercise 7: Nobody's Saying Anything

A. Brief description:
A class volunteer role-plays a client situation where silence is emphasized. The rest of the class assumes the social work role and verbally responds to the silent "client."

B. Objectives:
You will be able to:
1. Identify ways of responding to a client who is being silent.
2. Assess your own reactions to uncomfortable situations when a client is silent.
3. Demonstrate responses which are appropriate and potentially effective in such a situation.

C. Procedure:

1. Review the material on interviewing, especially that on silence in the interview and on doing the interview which is discussed in the text. It is also helpful to review related material on breast cancer, on HIV/AIDS, and on dealing with grief prior to undertaking the respective role play.[2]

2. After reading one of the following three client scenarios, the instructor will ask for a volunteer to play the role before the class. The volunteer will sit in the front of the class and respond as if she or he were the client.

   To avoid placing full responsibility for the social work role on any one individual, the worker role will be assumed on a general basis by the remainder of the class. Volunteers may jump in with responses they feel are appropriate. In the event that more than one person responds at the same time, the instructor will monitor the progression of turns.

Role-Play A: Silence and Breast Cancer

Client Role: Verbenia is devastated. She feels that her life has just begun—and now that it might be cut cruelly short. Verbenia knows she is worried and upset, but really doesn't want to talk about it. She views herself as a private person who doesn't feel comfortable sharing personal information, especially with strangers. Talking about her own breast, for heaven's sakes, is even worse.

Worker Role: You are a hospital social worker. Verbenia has been referred to you after her physician noted the presence of a breast lump during her annual exam. The procedure at this particular hospital's health clinic is to refer patients who are anxious about diagnoses to social workers for information and counseling.

Role-Play B: Silence and AIDS

Client Role: Hank has just learned that he is HIV positive. He had visited a confidential testing site two weeks ago and just got his results today. He has had numerous female sexual partners and figures that is how he contracted HIV. He's in such shock he can hardly talk.

(continued)

[2] The supplementary material for Role-Plays A and B is taken from C. Zastrow and K. Kirst-Ashman, *Understanding Human Behavior and the Social Environment* (Chicago: Nelson-Hall, 4th ed., 1997). The supplementary material for Role C is taken from chapter 7 of the text which addresses dealing with grief.

Worker Role: You work at a crisis intervention unit. People with problems come in off of the street for help. Hank just walked into the unit and was referred to you.

Role-Play C: Silence and Dealing with Grief

Client Role: Lois is interested in becoming a foster parent. She cannot have children herself and would love to contribute to other children's welfare if she can't to her own. The problem is that her father died a month ago. She was very close to him and can't seem to concentrate on anything else but her grief.

Worker Role: You are a placement worker for a state foster care unit. You are conducting an initial interview with Lois, a potential foster parent. The purpose of the interview is to find out some basic information about the person's life including marital status and relationships, family history, current work situation and history, personal interests, and emotional stability. Lois mentions that her father just died. She appears to be very upset about it. You feel it is an important aspect to investigate concerning her ability to function as a stable foster parent.

3. The client for the chosen role play should take her or his place at the front of the class. Class members should then take turns asking questions. This can proceed for fifteen to twenty minutes.
4. The instructor will intervene and begin a class discussion focusing on the following questions:
    a. Which techniques and responses demonstrated by class members appeared to be the most effective?
    b. Which techniques and responses didn't seem to work? What do you think were the reasons they didn't work?
    c. What did "social workers" find most difficult about this role play?
    d. What feelings and reactions did the client experience while doing the role play?
    e. How helpful was the information about breast cancer?
    f. What did you learn from this role play?

Exercise 8: Working with Difficult Clients

A. Brief description:
The class is divided into threes, and participants play a difficult client, a worker, and an observer.

B. Objectives:
You will be able to:
1. Demonstrate responses to difficult clients.
2. Assess the appropriateness and effectiveness of such responses.

C. Procedure:
1. Review the material in the text on confronting clients and involuntary clients.
2. Break up into groups of three. Each group member should take one of the three roles: client, worker, or observer.
3. The instructor will read the client role. Afterwards, the client and worker should participate in the role play, continuing the scene for about 10 minutes. Meanwhile, the observer should take notes about his or her impressions of what's going on. The worker role is school social worker.

Client Role

The client is a fourteen-year-old male named Horace. Horace has been referred to the school social worker because of frequent truancy and another student's accusation that Horace stole his expensive new jacket. Unconfirmed rumors have also been going around parts of the student body that Horace often brings a concealed 9 mm semiautomatic handgun to school. Horace has been seen in the company of a gang called the Toros Machos which has been growing in popularity among the school's students.

Horace is angry and annoyed that he's been called in to see the school "shrink" (as he calls the school social worker). He is not planning on cooperating unless he feels he has to. He comes in to see the school social worker.

4. The instructor will tell you to stop the role play after about ten minutes. Take another ten minutes to discuss the following questions:
   a. What techniques used by the worker were effective? For what reasons?
   b. What techniques used by the worker appeared ineffective? For what reasons?
   c. What suggestions do you have for improvement?
   d. What have you learned from this role play that you think you'll be able to apply to practice?
5. After approximately ten minutes, your instructor will call you back to participate in a large group discussion. Summarize what you concluded in your small groups.

Exercise 9: The Truth or Not the Truth? That Is the Question

A. Brief description:
Students role play client and worker, and the worker suspects the client is lying.

B. Objectives:
You will be able to:
1. Demonstrate responses to a client suspected of not telling the truth.
2. Assess the appropriateness and effectiveness of such responses.

C. Procedure:
1. Review the material on suspicion of untruth presented in the text.
2. Divide up into pairs. In each pair, decide who will play the client and worker first. The worker role is the client's probation officer. The client role is described below:

Client Role

Molly Coddle, twenty-three, is on parole. She was convicted of armed robbery, and spent the past two years in a state prison. She has a history of not showing up for appointments with her other prior parole and probation officers. One of the conditions of her parole is that she meet with her parole officer every week at a specified time. If she misses her appointment even once without an adequate excuse, she is to return to prison for six months. She missed last week's appointment.

Molly maintains that she called to say she couldn't make it and left a message. Due to a glitch in the system, voice mail was not working. Therefore, Molly says that she called the main desk, but doesn't know who answered the phone. The parole officer received no message. However, the secretary who usually answers the phone was sick last week. The agency got some temporary help that is now virtually impossible to track down in order to determine whether a message was left or not.

The parole officer is pulled between believing Molly's story and not believing her. Believing the story might better maintain the worker/client relationship. However, getting a reputation with other clients for being "easy" would be a disaster.

3. Participate in the role play for approximately 10 minutes. The worker should concentrate on two tasks:
   a. Label what is true and what does not appear to be true.
   b. Decide what to do about the situation.

   The client may creatively develop excuses. For instance, the client can elaborate on anything including flat tires, oversleeping, hemorrhoids acting up, helping a friend get an abortion, etc. The client should use both (hypothetically) factual and untrue statements to the probation officer.

4. After about ten minutes, the instructor will tell you to reverse roles for another ten minutes. Start from the beginning. The new client can develop his or her own set of excuses. The worker should concentrate on the same two tasks described above.
5. At the end of the second role play, the instructor will bring the class back to participate in a large class discussion. The following questions will be addressed:
   a. As worker, did you or did you not believe the client's excuses? What were your reasons?
   b. As worker, what techniques did you use to establish the truth? To what extent did these techniques work? What problems did you encounter?
   c. As client, what techniques did you feel the worker used which were exceptionally effective?
   d. As client, what techniques do you think would have proved more effective?
   e. What was the final decision about what to do in the role plays?
   f. As worker, how difficult was it to come to a decision?
   g. As client, do you feel the worker was fair or not?
   h. To what extent do you think this role play resembles possible real-life worker-client situations?
   i. What did you learn from this role play that you think you'll be able to apply to real practice situations?

3 Mezzo Practice Skills: Working with Groups

I. Introduction

II. Types of Groups

A. Task Groups

1. Board of directors

   a. Service is often challenging

   b. Members must use tact and finesse

   c. Are an irreplaceable asset for agency

2. Task forces

   a. Established for a special purpose and usually disbanded after completion of the task

   b. May be created by any other task group

3. Committees and commissions

   a. Committees: usually work in a particular area

      1) Standing committee: Exists on a continuous basis

      2) Ad hoc committee: Set up for one purpose and expected to cease operation after completing its task

   b. Commissions: usually ongoing in nature and responsible for a particular task

4. Legislative bodies

   a. Composed of elected representatives

b. Responsible for establishing laws and appropriating funds

c. Social workers may need to testify before them or serve as members of their commissions

d. Very important for social workers to be familiar with how they operate

5. Staff meetings

6. Multidisciplinary teams (M teams)

7. Case conferences and staffings

   a. Meet on an as-needed basis instead of regularly

8. Social action groups

   a. Social action: A coordinated effort to achieve institutional change to meet a need, solve a social problem, correct an injustice, or enhance the quality of human life

   Highlight 3.1: Social Action Within a University

9. Treatment groups

   a. Growth groups

      1) No presumption that members have a problem

      2) Worker is a facilitator

   b. Therapy groups

      1) Focus on correcting a problem and learning better problem-solving and coping styles

2) Worker role will be of higher visibility in the beginning and will probably become more of a facilitator as the group progresses

c. Educational groups

1) No presumption of a problem

2) Worker is often group leader throughout

d. Socialization groups

1) Presumption that members have a deficit of some sort in social skills

2) Worker role is one of highest visibility

e. Support groups (self-help groups)

1) No presumption of a problem

2) Self-help groups are less likely to have professional leadership

III. Worker Roles in Groups

A. Broker: Helps clients obtain needed resources by connecting them with community agencies

B. Mediator: Helps group members resolve conflicts or other dissension

C. Educator: Provides group participants with new information, structures presentations, and uses modeling to help members learn

D. Facilitator: Guides, eases, or expedites the way for others

IV. Basic Group Dynamics

A. Group Development

1. Four stages of development
    a. Stage 1: Strong reliance on leader
    b. Stage 2: Group members begin to assert themselves more
        1) Conflict is common
        2) Power and control issues become more frequent
        3) Leader should encourage open discussion of conflict
    c. Stage 3: Group productivity increases
        1) Working phase
        2) Trust is developed
        3) Worker's role will be more of consultant or advisor than director
    d. Stage 4: Separation
        1) Feelings of loss and maybe some anger

Highlight 3.2: Stages in Teen Group Therapy

B. Group Culture, Norms, and Power
1. Culture: Traditions, customs, and values/beliefs shared by group members
2. Norms: Unwritten expectations about how individuals will act in certain situations
3. Power: Issues always exist within groups

C. Group Size, Composition, and Duration

D. Decision Making in Groups

1. Decision making by consensus
    a. All members support and accept the decision even if they were not initially so inclined
    b. Requires atmosphere of openness
2. Decision making by compromise
    a. Reach a solution that most, if not all, members can support
    b. May not please anyone entirely but is viewed as the best that can be done
3. Decision making by majority
    a. Most deliberative bodies use this
    b. Over one-half support an idea
4. Rule by an individual
5. Persuasion by a recognized expert
6. Averaging of individual opinions
7. Persuasion by a minority

    Highlight 3.3: Approaches to Decision Making

    Highlight 3.4: Other Approaches to Decision Making

8. Nominal group technique
    a. Each member lists ideas
    b. Leader asks each member to provide one idea and continues until done, writing them on the board or flip chart
    c. Leader makes sure all members understand each idea

d. Each member is asked to prioritize to decrease the overall list by one-half or three-quarters

e. Leader places mark by each idea

f. Members rank the new list

g. Technique can produce a larger number of alternatives than most approaches

9. Brainstorming

10. Parliamentary procedure

a. *Robert's Rules of Order*

b. Filibuster: Endlessly speaking to prevent a group from conducting its business

c. Motions: Proposed actions that a group is asked to support

1) Primary motions: Bring business to the group for consideration

a) Main motions

b) Incidental motions, e.g., adjournment

2) Secondary motions

a) Used to act upon the primary motion

(1) Amend

(2) Refer to another body

(3) Defer action

b) Used to challenge improper actions and request information

(1) Point of order

(2) Point of information

3) "I call the question"

a) Motion not debatable

b) Halts discussion if supported by two-thirds of those present

d. Vote is recorded

1) Chair may vote to break a tie or to create a tie

2) If a tie occurs, the motion does not pass

e. Amendments

1) Voted first before main motion (with amendments) is voted on

f. Quorum: Minimum number of group members that must be present to conduct business

g. Minutes: Official record of group action

E. Group Roles

1. Task roles

a. Instructor

b. Information seeker

c. Opinion seeker

d. Evaluator

e. Elaborator

f. Energizer

g. Recorder

h. Procedural technician

2. Maintenance roles

a. Harmonizer

b. Compromiser

c. Encourager

d. Follower

e. Tension reliever

f. Listener

3. Nonfunctional roles

a. Aggressor

b. Blocker

c. Recognition seeker

d. Dominator

e. Help seeker

f. Confessor

g. Scapegoat

h. Defensive members

i. Deviant members

j. Quiet members

k. Internal leader

Figure 3.1: A Variety of Group Roles

V. Micro Skills in Groups

VI. Groups and the Generalist Intervention Model (GIM)

A. Engagement

B. Assessment

C. Planning

D. Implementation

E. Evaluation

F. Termination

G. Follow-Up

VII. Task and Treatment-Group Skills

A. Conflict Resolution

1. Recognizing conflict

Highlight 3.5: The Family Treatment Program: Recognizing Conflict

2. Assessing conflict

Highlight 3.6: That Is Not What I Said: Assessing Conflict

3. Choosing a strategy and intervening

Highlight 3.7: Square Peg in a Round Hole: Choosing a Strategy

a. Win-lose and win-win situations

4. Modeling and coaching

Highlight 3.8: Teaching Disciplinary Techniques: Modeling and Coaching

5. Team building

6. Confrontation

7. Consultation

   a. Case consultation: Focus is on a specific client or situation

   b. Program consultation: Focus on agency policies and practices instead of a specific client

8. Coordination

9. Using structure

VIII. Chapter Summary

EXPERIENTIAL EXERCISES AND SIMULATIONS

There are four exercises in this chapter, each designed to illustrate a concept or technique. The first exercise concerns brainstorming, a method of gathering ideas for making decisions in groups. Exercise 2 is an ice breaker typical of those which can be used to help members of a group become better acquainted at their first meeting. The third exercise is an activity in which you must make a group decision using the consensus model of decision making. Exercise 4 involves parliamentary procedure. It provides a role play which illustrates many of the motions and actions which occur in larger groups using *Robert's Rules of Order*.

Exercise 1: Brainstorming

A. Brief description:
You will be using the brainstorming procedure described in chapter 3 to generate ideas on a specific topic. Group members will be given instructions to follow. One member of the group will be responsible for leading the group in the exercise. Several groups will be operating simultaneously.

B. Objectives:
You will be able to:
   1. Use brainstorming to help a group develop multiple ideas on a topic.
   2. Recognize and follow the steps in the brainstorming process.

C. Procedure:
   1. You will be asked to play roles in the following vignette:

Vignette

You are members of the "Respect Diversity" task force on your campus. The task force is responding to a series of physical and verbal attacks directed at gay and lesbian students. Your responsibility is to provide the college president with a list of ideas on how the school can encourage respect for diversity on your campus. She has said that the school has a substantial budget to pursue this project and wants your group to give her all the help you can.

2. The instructor will assign one person to act as the group leader. That person will be responsible for ensuring that the group follows proper procedures. For example, this person will be responsible for ensuring that members do not stop to evaluate each idea and that all who wish to participate have an opportunity. Members should raise their hands before participating. The leader should encourage all contributions and clarify any ideas that are not clear. Additionally, the leader will write down the ideas generated by the group.
3. Remember that the goal is to generate as many ideas as possible. No attempt is made to rate or evaluate the ideas. Members should be free to present ideas they thought of after hearing other members' contributions.
4. The group leader begins by asking who wants to provide the first idea. She then writes the first idea on the board or flip chart provided by the instructor.
5. The group continues this process until all ideas have been collected.
6. After the brainstorming has ended, the entire class can discuss the following questions and issues:
    a. What are the positive aspects of using such a brainstorming technique?
    b. What are the negative aspects?
    c. What specifically would the task group present to the college president?
    d. Summarize the specific steps used in this brainstorming process.
    e. What other situations can you envision where brainstorming might be harmful?

Exercise 2: An Ice Breaker

A. Brief description:
Many groups begin with some sort of an ice breaker for helping members get to know one another better. The one described below is a nonthreatening activity which focuses on potential career choices.

B. Objectives:
You will be able to:
1. Learn about the interests of other members of your group.
2. Become familiar with one ice breaker which can be used with groups of various ages.

3. Become better acquainted with other group members.

C. Procedure:

1. Consider the fact that many people pursue a number of careers in their lives that are different from the one for which they were trained. Take a few minutes to jot down three careers which you have some interest in. Assume that you might be able to switch to any one of them at a later point in your life.
2. Next to each career write down the characteristic you find most attractive about this career.
3. Next, list a disadvantage or problem with that career.
4. Take turns going around the class in round-robin fashion, with each person describing her or his three choices together with the advantages and disadvantages of each. Other group members should be free to ask the person further questions about one or more of the careers they have selected.

Exercise 3: A Consensus Activity

A. Brief description:

You will have the opportunity to practice decision making by consensus. You will recall that the consensus model is used in groups to reach decisions with which all members are reasonably comfortable.

B. Objectives:

You will be able to:

1. Use a consensus model to reach decisions important to the group.
2. Understand why reaching consensus often takes longer than other decision-making approaches such as majority rule.

C. Procedure:

1. Divide the class into groups of four to five.
2. You will be asked to participate in the following role play:

Role Play

The social work program at your school must develop a retention policy that identifies the factors which would result in a student being counseled out of social work. The program is required to do this by its accreditation body, but faculty members want to have student input into the decision. As the student members of the program's advisory board, you have been asked to formulate at least five actions or behaviors which would warrant dismissal from social work.

Your fellow students have decided this is such an important activity that you must reach consensus on the five actions or behaviors. That is to say, you may not vote or otherwise decide based on majority opinion. Your input must reflect substantial agreement of all members.

3. Try to follow these guidelines in order to reach consensus:
   a. To make decisions by consensus requires an atmosphere of openness where all members have an opportunity to be heard and to influence the ultimate outcome.
   b. Each member should be able to present ideas without being criticized.
   c. Opposing views should be solicited and creative solutions encouraged.
   d. The emphasis is on finding the best solution instead of on getting one's way.
4. Select one member as both leader and recorder to help get the process underway. You might consider having each member contribute two ideas to the project, then rank-order each of the suggestions after discussing the merits and demerits of each.
5. Report your results back to the larger group.
6. The entire class can then pursue the following questions:
   a. How did your experience with consensus decision making compare with past decision-making activities in which you have been involved?
   b. What are some barriers to using a consensus model of decision making?
   c. What are the advantages to this method of making decisions?

Exercise 4: Parliamentary Procedure

A. Brief description:

This exercise is designed to familiarize you with the terminology and procedure used in groups operating under *Robert's Rules of Order*. The example given is of a social work student organization. Various roles are identified. Those playing the roles read the appropriate portions of the transcript.

B. Objectives:

You will be able to:

1. Recognize and use appropriate motions to conduct the business of an organization.
2. Understand what steps are needed to bring a matter up for discussion and vote by any group.

C. Procedure:

1. The instructor will assign specific roles to individual students (there are a total of eleven roles, plus those of members-at-large). Members-at-large will vote on all issues before the group.
2. The roles are: president, vice president, treasurer, secretary, chair of the activities committee, chair of the faculty relations committee, chair of the social action committee, and members 1, 2, 3, and 4.
3. Each person playing a role will read his or her script from the transcript of the meeting. It is important to stay alert and recognize your part.

4. Feel free at any point to ask the instructor about the purpose or meaning of any particular motion.
5. At the end of the role play, the class can discuss the following questions:
   a. Why is there such a seemingly rigid set of steps to be followed in parliamentary procedure (such as making a motion, seconding it, debating, and voting on it)?
   b. What steps in this process appear most confusing to you?
   c. Why does *Robert's Rules of Order* prevent a person who voted with the losing side from asking to have the matter reconsidered later?

Parliamentary Procedure Role Play
The Social Work Student Organization

President: The meeting of the Social Work Student Organization is called to order. The minutes of the April 1st meeting have been distributed. Is there a motion for approval?

Vice President: I move approval of the minutes of the April 1st meeting.

President: Is there a second?

Chair of Social Action Committee: I second the motion.

President: Is there any discussion?

Chair of Faculty Relations Committee: I think my motion last time was to ask the faculty to provide three spots on the advisory board for student representatives, not four as the minutes show.

Secretary: I think she's right. That appears to be a typo. It should have been three, not four.

President: Are there any more changes? If not, I'll ask for a vote to approve the minutes. All in favor of approving the minutes with the change noted, please say Aye.

All: Aye.

President: All opposed, please say no. The motion passes.

President: May we have the Treasurer's report, please.

(continued)

Treasurer: My report has also been distributed. It shows a balance of $240.04 after our car smash fund-raiser. We only had one bill and that was dry cleaning to get the oil out of Professor Mower's sportscoat from the car smash. He's such a good sport, he didn't even complain about the rest of his clothes. Are there any questions about the Treasurer's report?

President: A motion to accept the Treasurer's report is in order.

Member 1: I move to accept the Treasurer's report.

Member 2: I second the motion.

President: All in favor of the motion, please say Aye.

All: Aye.

President: All opposed?

President: The motion passes unanimously.

President: Does the Activity Committee have a report?

Chair of Activities Committee: Thank you. Yes, we do. The committee has organized the second Urban Plunge trip for the 29th of the month. We will be visiting Metropolis and spending the weekend in a homeless shelter. We will be leaving campus Friday at noon, working in the shelter Saturday and Sunday, and returning to campus Monday morning. We have room for two more people in the van. The cost is $25 plus a share of the gas. This looks like a good opportunity to learn more about the homeless first hand, and to talk to social workers from other agencies. Any questions?

Secretary: I'd like to move that our organization pay for the gas costs since we are sponsoring this activity.

President: It has been moved that SWSO pay for the gas for this trip. Is there a second?

Member 1: I second the motion.

President: Any discussion *(continued)*

Treasurer: I'd like to amend the motion to set a limit of $50 on the gas costs.

President: Is there a second? I don't hear a second so the amendment dies. Is there any further discussion on the original motion? Hearing none, all in favor of the motion, please say Aye.

All but Treasurer: Aye.

President: All opposed, say no.

Treasurer: No.

President: The motion carries. The Activities Committee will let the Treasurer know what the gas costs and he will reimburse you.

President: I believe the Social Action Committee has a report.

Chair of Social Action Committee: Yes, we do. We are in the final stages of planning for our social action day. At present, we have a speaker from the Gay and Lesbian Organization speaking on the latest campus problems faced by their members; another speaker from the Action Coalition, who will talk about how student organizations can join together to bring about social change; and a representative from the Chippewa Tribe, who will speak on tribal rights and history.

We have also planned a letter-writing to get the local paper and media to focus their attention on the *Cinco de Mayo* Chicano festival. We're working with the Chicano Student Organization on this project. Are there any questions?

President: Thanks for your report.

President: Is there any other old business?

Vice President: I move we disband the Social Action Committee. They're getting too radical for me.

President: You're out of order, Danforth, we already discussed and voted on that matter last time.

Vice President: I move to reconsider our previous decision. *(continued)*

Chair of Activities Committee: Point of order.

President: What is your point of order?

Chair of Activities Committee: Danforth voted with the losing side on that previous vote. He is not permitted to move for reconsideration. Only a person who voted on the winning side can make such a motion.

President: You are correct. Again, Danforth, your motion is out of order. Is there any new business?

Member 2: I move that we hold an end-of-year party, like last year.

Member 1: I second the motion.

President: It's been moved and seconded to have an end-of-year party. Is there discussion?

Member 3: Given the time of day, I move we refer this motion to the Activities Committee and ask them to report by our next meeting.

Member 4: I second the motion.

President: All in favor of referring the party idea to the Activities Committee say Aye.

All: Aye.

President: All opposed, say no.

President: The Ayes have it. This matter is referred to the Activities Committee. If there is no other business to come before us, I declare the meeting adjourned.

4 Macro Practice Skills: Working with Organizations and Communities

I. **Introduction**

II. **Defining Macro Practice**

A. Designed to Improve or Modify Some Aspect of Society

III. **The Organizational Context of Social Work Practice**

Highlight 4.1: When the Agency You Work For Is Part of the Problem

A. Professional-Organizational Conflicts

B. Limitations and Risk Assessment

IV. **Theoretical Base for Organizational and Community Change**

A. Organizational Theory

1. How the organization functions

2. What improves or impairs the ability of the organization to accomplish its mission

3. What motivates people to work toward organizational goals

B. Community Theory: Nature of communities and social work practice within communities

1. Social functions of communities

a. Production, distribution, and consumption of goods and services

b. Socialization

c. Social control

d. Social participation

e. Mutual support

C. Social Reform

1. Concerned with problems on a large scale and focuses efforts in legislative arenas

D. Social Action

1. Advocacy around specific populations and issues

2. Working in local and national elections to support these issues

3. Networking with other groups pursuing a similar agenda

Highlight 4.2: Community Organization: The Traditional Focus on the Community in Macro Practice

a. Social action

b. Social planning

c. Locality development

E. Cause Advocacy: Advocate on behalf of an issue of overriding importance to a group of clients; also called class advocacy

F. Case Advocacy: Advocate on behalf of a single case

V. Micro Skills for Organizational and Community Change

Highlight 4.3: Social Workers Can Help Improve Delivery of Services

VI. Mezzo Skills for Organizational and Community Change

Highlight 4.4: Saving a Community: A Task Group at Work

A. Conflict Resolution

B. Developing Win-Win Outcomes

C. Team Building

D. Public Speaking

E. Consultation

VII. Macro Skills for Organizational and Community Change

A. Evaluating Outcomes

1. Practice evaluation: Focus on the effectiveness or results of what individual social workers do

a. Single subject design

b. Task achievement scaling

c. Client satisfaction surveys

d. Goal attainment scaling or goal accomplishment

2. Program evaluation: Focus on the effectiveness and results of entire programs

a. Needs assessments

b. Evaluability assessments

c. Process analysis

d. Outcome analysis

e. Cost-benefit analysis

B. Fund-Raising

1. Individual donors

2. Corporate donors

3. Foundations

4. Membership dues

5. Benefits

C. Budgeting

1. Line-item budgets: Statement of expenditures for a designated time where each cost item is noted on a separate line

   a. Depicts how money will be spent without describing what the agency does

   b. Many social agencies use this method

2. Program budgets: Statement of expenditures where cost items are broken down according to programs the agency provides

   a. Also known as functional budget

   b. Uses same structure as line-item

   c. Also identifies functions of agency

Figure 4.1: Comparison of Line-Item and Program Budgets

3. Incremental budgets: Agency's budget from last year is used as a starting point for this year's budget

4. Zero-based budgets: Starts with no money

   a. Budget must be justified based on activities to be accomplished or goals to be reached

   b. Generally considered inappropriate in social service areas

D. Negotiating

1. Guidelines for effective negotiation

   a. Separate the problem from the people involved

b. Direct attention to the mutual interests of both parties and not to the positions they are taking

c. Devise new options that benefit both sides

d. Both sides must agree to use objective criteria for deciding an issue

E. Mediating

1. Both parties meet with a third party who serves as an impartial referee or peacemaker

F. Influencing Decision Makers

1. Petitioning: Collecting signatures on a document asking an organization or person to act in a particular manner

Highlight 4.5: Petitioning Works

2. Working with the media

a. Reach out to media

b. Build contacts within the media

c. Be certain you are authorized to speak for an organization or agency

d. Provide easy access for media representatives to contact you

e. Learn necessary timelines for all media

f. Do not play favorites

g. If media makes a mistake, consider your reactions with care

h. If message doesn't get reported, thank the reporters for their effort and indicate willingness to work with them again

3. Writing a press release

    a. Use the five W's: Who, What, When, Where, and Why

    b. First paragraph should include crucial information

    c. Follow up with a phone call

    Figure 4.2: Using the Media: An Example of a News Release

4. Educating

5. Persuading

    a. Issue consensus

    b. Issue difference

    c. Issue dissensus

6. Confrontation

    a. Legal action

    b. Public embarrassment

    Highlight 4.6: Embarrassing a Landlord

7. Collaborating: Two or more persons work together to serve a given client

    a Letter writing

    Highlight 4.7: Letter Writing Strategies

    b. Needs assessment

        1) Key informant approach

2) Community forum approach

3) Rates-under-treatment approach

4) Social indicators approach

5) Field study

G. Planning

1. Program Evaluation and Review Technique (PERT)

a. Identify major tasks to be accomplished

b. Place tasks in sequential order

c. Determine probable time needed for completion of each step

d. Identify those responsible for completing each task

Figure 4.3: A Sample Program Evaluation and Review Technique (PERT) Chart

H. Working with Coalitions

VIII. Worker Roles in Organizational and Community Change

A. Initiator: Calls attention to an issue

B. Negotiator: Represents organization with other groups

C. Advocate: Speaks out and acts on behalf of client

D. Spokesperson: Authorized to speak on behalf of others

E. Organizer: Coordinates individuals or groups to pursue some designated function(s)

F. Mediator: Resolves disagreement among various systems in conflict

G. Consultant: Provides advice, suggestions, or ideas for another person, group, or organization

IX. Generalist Intervention Model (GIM) in Macro Practice

A. Engagement

B. Assessment

C. Planning

D. Implementation

E. Evaluation

X. Chapter Summary

EXPERIENTIAL EXERCISES AND SIMULATIONS

The three exercises for this chapter are designed to accomplish two purposes. One is to provide experience in two of the methods used to influence decision makers: using the media and letter writing. The second purpose is to help identify the primary methods workers use in pursuing organizational and community change.

Exercise 1: Preparing a Press Release

A. Brief description:
In this exercise, you will prepare a press release about the opening of a new agency. You will work on this as a task group.

B. Objectives:
You will be able to:
1. Develop a news release suitable for dissemination to newspapers, radio, or television.
2. Identify the key items which should appear in every news release.

C. Procedure:
1. There are a number of reasons why you might write a news release for your agency. These include announcement of a new service provided by the agency, the need to publicize an existing program, or a desire to recruit volunteers or foster parents. Working with and using the news media to publicize events, activities, and perspectives is an essential skill. News releases are one of the easiest and simplest ways to keep the media informed about your agency or activity. As in any news article, basic

information is expected by the reader. This includes such items as who, what, where, why, when, and how.

2. Break down into work groups of two or three persons.
3. Read the following example of an agency news release. It was written to publicize the creation of a new program and provides information about services provided, hours of operation, and contact persons.

> Rural Mental Health Clinic
> 12 East North Street
> East North Overshoe, Vermont
> 802/658-0371
>
> For Immediate Release:
>
> Drug and Alcohol Program a First in State
>
> EAST NORTH OVERSHOE, VT—December 28, 1998, The Rural Mental Health Clinic has added a drug and alcohol program to its new service center in East North Overshoe.
>
> According to the Director, Jim Beam, the new program is the first in the state to offer both inpatient and outpatient service to chemically addicted individuals. The clinic has added three staff members and will be hosting an open house on Friday, January 14, from 1:00-3:00 p.m. The office for the new program is at 232 Spring Street.
>
> For further information, contact Jim Beam at 658-0371 or 658-9981.

4. Now prepare your own news release. Put yourself in the following role:

> **Scenario**
>
> You are the director of a new agency established to coordinate services to families in Clearwater City. Your agency was set up through the cooperative efforts of four existing agencies which felt they could better serve families in need by pooling their resources. You want the community to know about your agency and about the fact that several agencies acted cooperatively to launch this program. You also want them to know that taxpayers' money is being used in a positive fashion.
>
> There is only one newspaper in your city, the *Daily Planet*, and no other print media. There is a radio station that plays funeral dirges all day and does not have any news programs. Their only public service announcements cover the openings of new mortuaries and the daily obituaries. Plan your news release to convey information succinctly and in an interesting manner.

5. In the release, remember to include the following elements:
   a. *Who* (person or agency) is this news release about?
   b. *What* is important enough to deserve a news article?
   c. *When* did or will this event occur?
   d. *Where* or in what location did this event occur?
   e. *Why* is this being brought to the attention of the public?
   f. *How* did this event occur?

   The entire release should be no longer than one page. Take about 20 minutes to write it. Remember that, although this release will be handwritten for the purposes of this assignment, a real release would be typewritten, double-spaced, with margins of at least 1 ½ inches on each side of the page.
6. After you complete your release, your instructor may ask you to share what you've written with the entire class. The class may address the following questions:
   a. What are the similarities among the various releases?
   b. What are the differences?
   c. What did you find most difficult about writing the release?
   d. Describe in your own words how such a news release might benefit the agency for which you work.

Exercise 2: Letter Writing

A. Brief description:
There are many ways to influence decision makers. One method is to write to them, expressing your opinions and ideas. This exercise will give you practice in writing a business letter.

B. Objectives:
You will be able to:
1. Prepare a business letter which contains appropriate items such as the correct opening, closing, presentation of ideas, etc.
2. Recognize inappropriate format in a business letter.

C. Procedure:
1. Review the instructions for writing a letter shown below. They are taken from Highlight 4.7 in the text.

Letter Writing Strategies

To be effective, letters:
a. Are planned carefully, revised, polished, and proofread;
b. Include letterhead (with address), date, salutation (Dear ___), body, complimentary close (Sincerely), and both typed and written signature;
c. Are businesslike and pleasant;
d. Are brief (preferably one page) and discuss only one topic;
e. Open with a positive comment; *(continued)*

f. Are factual, and simply written;
g. Should have perfect grammar and spelling; and
h. Request a response.

Letters which are less likely to be effective include those that appear identical, those copied out of newspaper advertisements, or clearly mass-produced letters (e.g., duplicated copies instead of original). Letters which attack the reader are less likely to work and may backfire. Some people advocate handwritten letters, but the advantages of a clear, typed message outweigh the advantages of a handwritten communication.

If letters are to be mass produced, as might be desired when a group is trying to sway the reader, at least vary the letters so that they don't appear identical. Written letters are helpful in certain situations and help create a record of communication with the decision maker. They should be used as an adjunct to, and not instead of, other more personal forms of contact. Person-to-person communication is still superior to written messages as a means of influencing other people.

2. Now read the business letter shown below. In a number of ways, it is very poorly constructed.

January 31, 1998

Mr. Raul Prenner
Department of Aging
1492 Columbus Way
Santa Maria, NY 00923

Dear Mr. Prenner:

You've got your nerve telling my client she isn't eligible for your program. I don't know how you get off with your attitude. It's really poor. My client and I think you need to change your policy so that people like my client can use your agency.

I think we need to get together to talk about your silly policies at my earliest convenience. Please call my office and arrange for an appointment immediately.

Yours Truly,

Edgar J. Hoover
Social Worker

3. List the things that are wrong with this letter. This may include the tone of the letter and the absence of important information.
4. Now rewrite this letter using the same general information contained in the poorly written letter. This time, use your own name and address. Be careful to conform to the standards for effectiveness described.
5. After completing the letters, the entire class can discuss the results. Address the following questions.
   a. In what specific ways was the original letter poorly written?
   b. In what specific ways could the original letter be improved?
   c. What things were the most difficult about writing your own letter?
   d. What might be some of the reasons for writing letters in social work practice?

Exercise 3: Connecting Roles and Responsibilities

A. Brief description:
Social workers may assume many roles in organizational and community change. Roles involve expectations regarding how you should behave and what you wish to accomplish. Learning these roles is not always easy. This exercise is designed to assist you in understanding and distinguishing the various roles which you may be called upon to play.

B. Objectives:
You will be able to:
1. Correctly identify several roles used by social workers pursuing organizational or community change.
2. Recognize major responsibilities associated with each of these roles.

C. Procedure:
1. Review the two columns shown below. In one column are the role titles frequently associated with change efforts in communities and organizations. In the second column are descriptions of various roles.

Role Titles	**Role Descriptions**
A. Initiator	1. Decides what the client is entitled to and what is keeping the client from receiving what she needs. Requires worker to assess an adversary's strengths and weaknesses.
B. Negotiator	2. Represents an organization or group trying to gain something from another group. Seeks win-win situations and a middle ground that both sides can accept.

(continued)

C. Advocate	3. Calls attention to an issue such as a problem existing in the community, an unmet need, or a situation to be improved.
D. Spokesperson	4. Helps two sides work out a compromise. The role player is neutral, not siding with either party. One task involves ensuring that both sides understand the other's positions.
E. Organizer	5. Provides advice, suggestions, or ideas to another person, group, or organization. Two characteristics are important: knowing more than the person being helped; and the ability to see her advice ignored without getting personally involved or hurt.
F. Mediator	6. Presents an organization's views to others without coloring them with his or her own opinions.
G. Consultant	7. Creates groups of people who share a similar concern. Tasks include developing the leadership potential of others, stimulating others to act, and identifying targets for change.

2. Match the Role Titles with the Role Descriptions.
3. Your instructor will supply you with the correct answers. Compare your answers with the correct ones.
4. Discuss the following questions with the entire class:
   a. What roles were the most difficult for you to understand?
   b. Describe possible agency situations where each role might be used.
   c. What are examples of practice situations in which workers might assume more than one role?
   d. Are there situations in which workers might have to assume roles that conflict with each other? If so, how might these roles conflict?

5 Engagement and Assessment in Generalist Practice

I. **Introduction**

II. **Engagement**

A. Greeting the Client

B. Demonstrating Effective Attending Skills

1. Listen carefully

2. Make eye contact

a. Be aware of cultural differences

3. Focus on client thoughts and feelings

a. Use open-ended questions

4. Use silence as necessary

5. Take notes of information you are unlikely to remember

C. Discussing Agency Services and Client Expectations

D. Deciding If the Agency and Worker Can Help

E. Offering Agency and Worker Services to the Client

F. Orienting the Client to the Helping Process

1. Client needs to know the rules and conditions

2. Negotiate with clients as to frequency of sessions, time and place, and total number of sessions

G. Completing Required Paperwork

III. Assessment

A. Acquire an understanding of a problem or issue, what causes it, and what can be changed to minimize or resolve it

Highlight 5.1: The Difference Between Diagnosis and Assessment

1. Diagnosis: patient's problems viewed as being inside the patient

2. Four ways assessment differs from diagnosis:

    a. Environmental surroundings considered as important as micro aspects

    b. Outside systems can become targets of change

    c. Emphasis on working *with client*, not *on client*

    d. Focus on strengths.

B. How to Approach Assessment

1. Micro

2. Mezzo

3. Macro

4. Human diversity

5. Each dimension requires focus on clients' problems and needs and on clients' strengths

Figure 5.1: Assessment in the Generalist Intervention Model (GIM)

C. Five Major Points

1. Involvement of client is absolutely essential

2. Assessment always involves making judgments

3. Highlighting strengths is paramount

4. A single, clear definition of the problem may not exist
5. Assessment is a continuous activity

Figure 5.2: Assessment in Planned Change Is an Ongoing Process

D. Goals of Assessment
   1. Articulate a clear statement of the problem
   2. Formulate a clear description of the client system
   3. Illustrate how the client system functions with other interacting systems
   4. Put all the information together

E. Assessment From a Micro Practice Perspective
   1. Defining problems and issues
      a. Recognize the client's unmet needs
      b. Identify the blocks to need fulfillment
      c. Formulate the problem in terms of removing blocks to need fulfillment
   2. Types of problems
      a. Interpersonal conflict
      b. Dissatisfaction in social relations
      c. Problems with formal organizations
      d. Difficulties in role performance
      e. Problems of social transition
      f. Psychological and behavioral problems
      g. Inadequate resources

h. Problems in decision making

i. Cultural conflicts

j. Prioritizing problems

F. Empowerment: Identifying Clients' Strengths

1. Family and friends
2. Education and employment background
3. Problem-solving and decision-making skills
4. Personal qualities and characteristics
5. Physical and financial resources
6. Attitudes and perspectives
7. Miscellaneous other strengths

G. Which Problem Should You Work On?

1. Client must recognize that the problem exists
2. Problems should be clearly defined
3. You and client should realistically be able to do something to remedy the problem
4. Partialization: Breaking down a problem or series of problems into manageable parts

Highlight 5.2: Examples of Questions You Can Ask During Assessment

H. Gathering Information: Sources of Assessment Data

1. Agency forms completed by client
2. Responses by clients to your questions during interview
3. Nonverbal behavior of client

4. Client's interactions with other people

5. Outside sources

6. Psychological or other testing

7. Your own interactions with client

I. Assessment Instruments

1. Diagnostic and Statistical Manual (DSM)

a. Five major axes:

1) Clinical disorders and conditions not directly attributable to a mental disorder

2) Personality disorders

3) Physical conditions

4) Environmental and psychosocial problems

5) Global assessment of overall level of functioning

b. Four reasons why DSM is relevant to social workers

1) Provides means for variety of professionals to communicate with each other

2) Helpful in evaluating and treating clients with mental disorders

3) Utility in teaching about mental disorders

4) Provides better opportunities to do research on mental disorders

c. Reasons to be wary of using DSM

1) Only describes particular conditions

2) Some tendency to focus on individual pathology instead of client interactions with the environment

3) Imperfections in its categories

2. Assessing Assertiveness

Figure 5.3: The Rathus Assertiveness Schedule (RAS)

3. Assessing alcohol and other drug abuse

Figure 5.4: An Alcoholism Test

J. Family Assessment

K. Choosing to Work with Families

L. Family Assessment Skills

1. Family communication
2. Family structure
3. Life-cycle adjustments
4. Impacts of the social environment
5. Key areas of family conflict

M. Family Relationships

Figure 5.5: Eco-Map

Figure 5.6: Genogram

N. Home Visits

1. Workers' reactions
2. Scheduling home visits
3. Taking care of your own safety

Highlight 5.3: Be Alert, Streetwise, and Safe

a. Elementary street sense

b. Walking smart

c. Elevator sense

d. Defensive driving

e. Tips for buses

f. If you are threatened

O. Assessment in Mezzo Practice: Assessing Groups

1. Potential sponsorship

2. Who should be members of the group?

Highlight 5.4: Sociograms

a. Selection criteria for treatment group membership

1) Motivation

2) Group purpose

3) Common communication skills

4) Group advantages versus disadvantages

b. Gathering information about potential treatment group members

1) Interviews with potential group members prior to beginning the group

2) Use of self-rating tests

c. Selection criteria for task group membership

1) Individual interests

2) Expertise

3) Homogeneity versus heterogeneity

4) Prestige in the community

5) Relationship with sponsoring agency

6) Diversity and demographic characteristics

d. Recruiting task group members

3. Ongoing group assessment

a. Individual self-rating questionnaires

b. Clients may keep diaries of daily events

c. Charting their improvements

d. Role-playing

e. Bring in outside observers

P. Assessment in Macro Practice

1. Assessment of community needs

a. Information

b. Resources available

c. State of program development

d. Community attitudes

2. An example of a community assessment

Highlight 5.5: A Format for Analyzing a Community or Neighborhood

a. Community characteristics

b. Community life

c. Available social services

d. Summary

3. Four-step needs assessment process

a. Step 1: Exploring the nature of the neighborhood

b. Step 2: Getting to kow the area and it's residents

c. Step 3: Identifying the community's strengths

d. Step 4: Talking to people in the community

4. Interviewing persons in the community

a. Take time for "chit-chat"

b. Provide a clear definition of your purpose

c. Clearly explain what community of people or neighborhood you are interested in

d. Get leads from your interviewee

e. Use micro skills

f. Get the specific information you need

g. Make sure interviewee has opportunity to share opinions and to conclude the interview

IV. Chapter Summary

EXERIENTIAL EXERCISES AND SIMULATIONS

The following exercises address various aspects of engagement and assessment. Exercise 1 looks at some typical mistakes made during engagement. Exercise 2 provides a case example with which to practice the assessment process. Exercise 3 presents the opportunity to practice assessing minor personal problems. Established assessment mechanisms on assertiveness and alcoholism are employed respectively in Exercises 4 and 5. Exercises 6 and 7 provide opportunities to practice, respectively, making genograms and eco-maps. Finally, Exercise 8 provides the opportunity to do a community analysis.

Exercise 1: Engagement

A. Brief description:
Working singly or as a group, students will identify problems in the engagement phase of a case example.

B. Objectives:
You will be able to:
1. Identify social worker errors in the engagement phase.
2. Describe appropriate worker actions in the engagement phase.

C. Procedure:
Read the brief vignette below. Identify at least five errors or problems on the part of the worker. Explain what the worker should have done to conduct an effective engagement.

Vignette

“Hi, Mary. I’m Derrick, your social worker here at the homeless shelter. I bet you really could use a shower and a meal.” With those opening statements, Derrick Broder greeted Mary Livingston, a woman who had just sought shelter for herself and her child.

“As you probably know, we don’t charge too much here and you’ll be glad you came to the shelter. We help lots of people with your problems.”

“Well, I don’t know,” said Mary. “I don’t have much money.”

“Don’t worry about a thing, Mary. Now lets get you and your little boy a bed and a meal. In the morning, I’ll have my colleague, Monica, meet with you to discuss ways you can improve your child-rearing skills, too. You’ll like her.”

Exercise 2: The Assessment Process

A. Brief description:
Students will break up into pairs and role play as worker and client, following the prescribed assessment process.

B. Objectives:
You will be able to:
1. Identify the steps in the assessment process.
2. Demonstrate a simulated case assessment.

C. Procedure:
1. Before beginning the exercise, review the material in the text on how to approach assessment, and on assessment from a micro practice perspective. A copy of the figure entitled “Assessment in the Generalist Intervention Model” is provided below. Follow these steps in your role play.

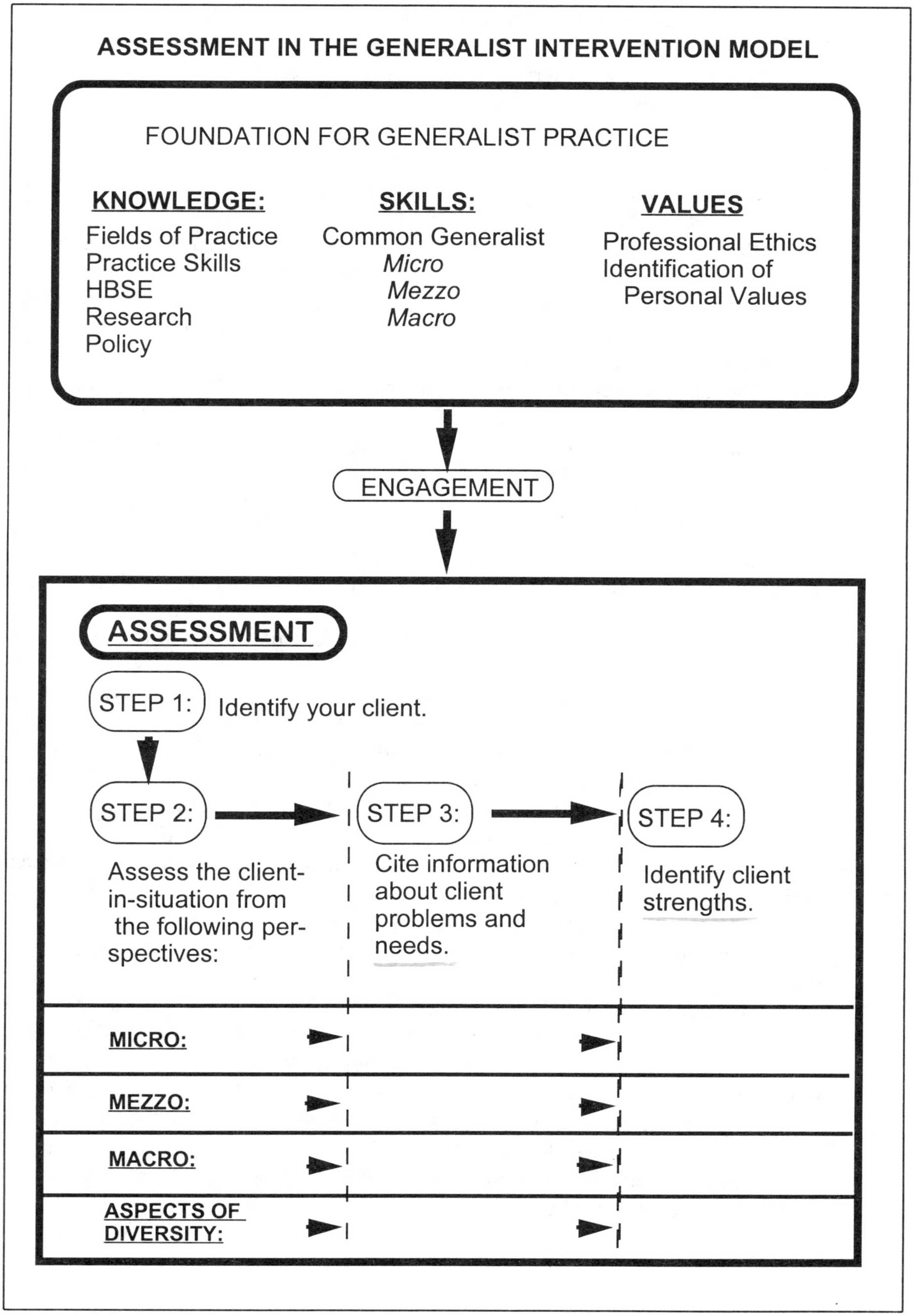
ASSESSMENT IN THE GENERALIST INTERVENTION MODEL
FOUNDATION FOR GENERALIST PRACTICE
KNOWLEDGE:
Fields of Practice
Practice Skills
HBSE
Research
Policy
SKILLS:
Common Generalist
Micro
Mezzo
Macro
VALUES
Professional Ethics
Identification of Personal Values
ENGAGEMENT
ASSESSMENT
STEP 1:
Identify your client.
STEP 2:
Assess the client-in-situation from the following per-spectives:
STEP 3:
Cite information about client problems and needs.
STEP 4:
Identify client strengths.
MICRO:
MEZZO:
MACRO:
ASPECTS OF DIVERSITY:

2. Divide up into pairs. One student in each pair will role play the client and the other the worker. The worker's task is to do an assessment of an elderly client as described below. The worker's job is intake worker for Horseradish County Social Services Department.

THE CLIENT

A concerned neighbor referred Grafton, seventy-seven, to the Horseradish County Elderly Protective Services Unit. Grafton lives on his rundown family farm on the outskirts of the rural Midwestern county. The neighbor reported that twice he found Grafton had fallen while walking out to get his mail, and the elderly man lay helplessly on the ground. Both times the neighbor had to practically carry Grafton back into the house. Grafton has rheumatoid arthritis, which makes it very difficult to walk even with his two canes. Additionally, his eyesight is very poor. The neighbor also raised questions about Grafton's ability to shop and cook for himself.

Grafton's wife, Vicki, died two years ago after a long bout with intestinal cancer. Since her death, Grafton has remained isolated and alone. He has three sons. Only his oldest son, Ralph, forty-eight, lives nearby in a small town in Horseradish County. He owns a small pea canning factory. Ralph works long hours to keep his business afloat and has little time to spend with his own family, let alone with Grafton. Ralph and his second wife, Janet, have three teenage children.

Grafton's second son, Chuck, forty-two, is a pop artist in San Francisco. The youngest, Jim, thirty-five, is a worm farmer in Idaho. Both are single.

Grafton considers himself an intelligent, independent man who worked hard all of his life to make his farm successful. However, since his arthritis took a turn for the worse ten years ago, he has had to stop actively farming. He is now facing financial difficulties. He's experienced many years of little income and high health costs for both himself and his wife. He is becoming increasingly depressed at his failing health. However, he clings doggedly to the notion that he must remain on his farm. To do otherwise, he thinks to himself, would mean giving up and accepting certain death. Grafton is aware of the Happy Hunting Ground Health Care Center, the only nursing home in the area. He has sadly watched some of his friends enter it, and dreads the thought of having to do himself.

In summary, Grafton's problems include: failing health involving arthritis, poor eyesight, and intestinal distress (the last of which he does *not* like to talk about); loneliness; having few activities to keep him busy; and feeling unwanted and unimportant. Strengths include: intelligence; independence; ownership of the farm; having concerned children; and an outgoing, sociable personality. Some of Grafton's likes include: a love of reading classical novels (on bright days when his eyesight improves slightly); seeing his children; playing stud poker; and drinking beer.

3. The worker should follow the assessment process as described in the text. Notes should be taken as if the worker would have to write up an actual assessment report. The role-played interview should last from fifteen to twenty minutes. The worker may choose to focus on the following:
   a. Acknowledgement of the specific problems and issues involved.
   b. Identification of the actual pros and cons of remaining in his own home versus entering a nursing home.
   c. Emphasis on Grafton's strengths and how he might best put them to use.
   d. Micro, mezzo, and macro aspects of the situation and how they might be involved.
   e. Aspects of diversity which might be important.

   The worker might choose to ask questions resembling the following:
   a. "What do you plan to do regarding your health problems?"
   b. "What do you feel you need at this time?"
   c. "Would you be interested in trying . . . ?"
   d. "How could you structure your time so that you'd be more able to do what you want to?" (See the figure in the text for additional questions to ask during assessment.)

   The person playing Grafton should feel free to elaborate on the information provided above and add detail. Grafton's description should be merely a starting point.
4. After fifteen to twenty minutes, your instructor will call you back for a class discussion. Focus on the following questions:
   a. What information that you collected do you think would be the most helpful in planning with a client such as Grafton?
   b. What information was the most difficult to obtain?
   c. What were your feelings about doing the interview, either as client or worker?
   d. What did you learn about assessment from participating in this role play?

Exercise 3: Peer Assessment

A. Brief description:
   In pairs, you will take turns assessing minor problems using the model proposed in the text.
B. Objectives:
   You will be able to:
   1. Identify the steps in the assessment process.
   2. Recognize how a personal problem can be assessed using the proposed process.
   3. Demonstrate the assessment of a problem.

C. Procedure:

1. Before beginning the exercise, review the material in the text on how to approach assessment, and on assessment from a micro practice perspective. Pay particular attention to figure 5.1, which portrays a figure entitled "Assessment in the Generalist Intervention Model," as you will be asked to follow these steps. A copy of this figure is provided in Exercise 2 above.
2. Specify to yourself some minor problem you are currently experiencing. It should be nothing too personal as you will be asked to share it with a partner.
3. Divide up into pairs. Take turns portraying the person describing a problem and the person doing the assessment. Take fifteen minutes each to answer questions concerning your problem asked by the "assessor." The assessor in each instance should follow the assessment format provided in the text. She or he should take notes as if preparing to write up a report.
4. After fifteen minutes your instructor will ask you to switch roles. After another fifteen minutes your instructor will call you back for a full class discussion.
5. Address the following questions:
   a. What information that you collected do you think would be the most helpful in planning a solution to the problem?
   b. What information was the most difficult to obtain?
   c. What were your feelings about doing the interview, either as assessor or client?
   d. What did you learn about assessment from participating in this role play?

Exercise 4: Are You Assertive?

A. Brief description:
You will complete the Rathus Assertiveness Questionnaire to evaluate your own assertiveness. You will then relate your findings to how similar assessment information may be used in actual practice.

B. Objectives:
You will be able to:

1. Identify some of the issues involved in assertive behavior.
2. Relate this information to assessment in practice situations.

C. Procedure:

1. Before beginning the exercise, review the material in the text on assessment instruments.

2. Take the Rathus Assertiveness Schedule (RAS) printed below.[1]

The Rathus Assertiveness Schedule (RAS)

Directions: Indicate how characteristic or descriptive each of the following statements is of you by using the code given below.

+3	Very characteristic of me, extremely descriptive
+2	Rather characteristic of me, quite descriptive
+1	Somewhat characteristic of me, slightly descriptive
-1	Somewhat uncharacteristic of me, slightly nondescriptive
-2	Rather uncharacteristic of me, quite nondescriptive
-3	Very uncharacteristic of me, extremely nondescriptive

____ 1. Most people seem to be more aggressive and assertive than I am.

____ 2. I have hesitated to make or accept dates because of shyness.

____ 3. When the food served at a restaurant is not done to my satisfaction, I complain about it to the waiter or waitress.

____ 4. I am careful to avoid hurting other people's feelings, even when I feel that I have been injured.

____ 5. If a salesman has gone to considerable trouble to show me merchandise which is not quite suitable, I have a difficult time in saying "no."

____ 6. When I am asked to do something, I insist upon knowing why.

____ 7. There are times when I look for a good and vigorous argument.

____ 8. I strive to get ahead as well as most people in my position.

____ 9. To be honest, people often take advantage of me.

____ 10. I enjoy starting conversations with new acquaintances and strangers.

____ 11. I often don't know what to say to attractive persons of the opposite sex.

____ 12. I will hesitate to make phone calls to business establishments and institutions.

____ 13. I would rather apply for a job or for admission to a college by writing letters than by going through with personal interviews.

(continued)

---

[1] The Rathus Assertiveness Schedule and the accompanying scoring explanation are adapted from "Rathus Assertiveness Schedule: Normative and Factor-Analytic Data," by D.B. Hull and J.H. Hull, *Behavior Therapy*, 9 (September, 1978), p. 673. Reprinted with permission of the authors and the Association for the Advancement of Behavior Therapy, 15 W. 36th St., New York, NY 10018.

____	14.	I find it embarrassing to return merchandise.
____	15.	If a close and respected relative were annoying me, I would smother my feelings rather than express my annoyance.
____	16.	I have avoided asking questions for fear of sounding stupid.
____	17.	During an argument I am sometimes afraid that I will get so upset that I will shake all over.
____	18.	If a famed and respected lecturer makes a statement which I think is incorrect, I will have the audience hear my point of view as well.
____	19.	I avoid arguing over prices with clerks and salesmen.
____	20.	When I have done something important or worthwhile, I manage to let others know about it.
____	21.	I am open and frank about my feelings.
____	22.	If someone has been spreading false and bad stories about me, I see him (her) as soon as possible to "have a talk" about it.
____	23.	I often have a hard time saying "no."
____	24.	I tend to bottle up my emotions rather than make a scene.
____	25.	I complain about poor service in a restaurant and elsewhere.
____	26.	When I am given a complaint, I sometimes just don't know what to say.
____	27.	If a couple near me in a theater or at a lecture were conversing rather loudly, I would ask them to be quiet or to take their conversation elsewhere.
____	28.	Anyone attempting to push ahead of me in a line is in for a good battle.
____	29.	I am quick to express an opinion.
____	30.	There are times when I just can't say anything.

3. Score the RAS by following these procedures:
   a. Change the sign from positive (+) to negative (–) or from negative (–) to positive (+) for your answers to the following questions:
      2, 4, 5, 9, 11, 12, 13, 14, 15, 16, 17, 19, 23, 24, 26, 30.
   b. Add up your total.
      1) Scores of –90 to –20 means you're generally unassertive, and probably too much so. The lower your score, the less assertive you are.
      2) Scores of –20 to +60 indicate you're within the realm of being appropriately assertive much of the time.
      3) Scores of +60 to +90 mean you're very assertive or possibly aggressive. This is a warning category.

|--------------------------|-------------------|-----------------------|

-90	-20	+60	+90
Unassertive	Assertive		Very Assertive Maybe Aggressive

4. Join a class discussion that addresses the following questions:
   a. How assertive does the RAS indicate you are?
   b. Do you think the RAS is accurate?
   c. What did you learn about assertiveness and assertive behavior by taking the RAS?
   d. What did you learn about improving assertiveness and assertive behavior by taking the RAS?
   e. For what types of client problems and needs might the RAS be used in practice?

Exercise 5: An Alcoholism Test

A. Brief description:
You will be asked to complete a test designed to provide a rough measure of alcoholism. You will then relate your findings as to how similar assessment information may be used in actual practice.

B. Objectives:
You will be able to:
1. Identify some of the issues involved in alcoholic behavior.
2. Relate this information to assessment in practice situations.

C. Procedure:
1. Before beginning the exercise, review the material on assessment instruments provided in the text.
2. Complete the following alcoholism test.

An Alcoholism Test[2]

Please honestly answer the following questions about your use of alcohol and other drugs:

1. Have you ever tried or decided to stop drinking or using drugs for a week or so only to find that this lasted a couple of days?
   Yes ____ No ____
2. Do you think people pay too much attention to how much you drink or use drugs?
   Yes ____ No ____
3. Have you ever switched brands of alcohol or types of drugs in an effort to control your use?
   Yes ____ No ____

(continued)

---

[2] This material is adapted from Norman K. Denzin, *Treating Alcoholism* (Newbury Park, CA: Sage, 1987), pp. 128-129. Reprinted by permission of Sage Publications, Inc., Newbury Park, CA 91320.

4. Do you need a drink or a drug to get started in the morning?
Yes ____ No ____
5. Do you admire people who can control drugs and alcohol?
Yes ____ No ____
6. Have you had problems with drugs and alcohol during the past year?
Yes ____ No ____
7. Has your drinking or use of drugs ever caused you problems at home with your family?
Yes ____ No ____
8. Do you take a few drinks before you go to parties, or try to get extra drinks at a party?
Yes ____ No ____
9. Do you tell yourself you can stop drinking any time you want to, even though you keep getting drunk when you drink?
Yes ____ No ____
10. Have you missed days at work or school because of your drinking or use of drugs?
Yes ____ No ____
11. Do you have "blackouts"; that is, are there times when you were drinking or using drugs which you cannot remember, or things that happened to you while you were drinking that you can't account for?
Yes ____ No ____
12. Have you ever had the feeling that your life would be better if you stopped using and drinking?
Yes ____ No ____
13. Do you hide alcohol?
Yes ____ No ____
14. Do you drink alone?
Yes ____ No ____
15. Do you feel guilt and remorse after you drink and use, or after a night of heavy drinking?
Yes ____ No ____
16. Have you ever been to a hospital or institution because of your drinking or use of drugs?
Yes ____ No ____

If you answer yes four or more times, you are probably in trouble with alcohol and drugs. (This test is a combination of questions contained on the National Alcoholism Test and in the twelve questions A.A. asks in its short pamphlet "Is A.A. for You?").

4. Join a class discussion that addresses the following questions:
   a. What did you learn about alcoholism and alcoholic behavior by taking the test?
   b. What practice situations might you envision where such a test might prove useful?
   c. How do you think clients might react to such a test?

Exercise 6: Genogram

A. Brief description:
Working independently, students will prepare a genogram of their own families.

B. Objectives:
You will be able to:
1. Construct a genogram with appropriate symbols.
2. Increase your awareness of your family history.

C. Procedure:
Review the description and examples of a genogram contained in the text. Interview family members and other data sources to gather the information you require. Construct a genogram of your family. What can you conclude from your review of this genogram?

Exercise 7: Eco-map

A. Brief description:
Students will prepare an eco-map for themselves or a friend. This can be done in class or as an out-of-class assignment.

B. Objectives:
You will be able to:
1. Construct an eco-map.
2. Increase your awareness of the information needed to construct eco-maps.

C. Procedure:
Review the description of eco-maps in the text. Using yourself or a friend or fellow student, construct an eco-map using appropriate symbols. Describe any patterns or unusual characteristics you noted when preparing the eco-map.

Exercise 8: Community Analysis

A. Brief description:
Small groups analyze the community your campus is in by following a prescribed format.

B. Objectives:
You will be able to:

1. Recognize the broad range of variables you need to assess in order to understand a community.
2. Apply a format for community analysis to the community where your campus is located.

C. Procedure:

1. Before beginning this exercise, review the material on assessment in macro practice provided in the text.
2. Break up into small groups of four to six persons.
3. Focusing on the community where your campus is located, take about forty-five minutes to begin answering the "Format for Analyzing a Community or Neighborhood"[3] cited below. It addresses community characteristics and community life. Additionally, it assesses the public welfare and social service system available in the community.

   Answer the questionnaire to the best of your ability. One group member should be assigned to take notes so that results can be discussed later with the entire class.

A Format for Analyzing a Community or Neighborhood

Below is a prescribed format for analyzing a community. It addresses community characteristics and community life. Additionally, it assesses the public welfare and social service system available in the community. Suggestions for undergoing the process of assessing a community have already been provided. Now we will provide a format for the specific types of questions to ask and for how to organize that information.

The questions asked in the various sections are not exhaustive nor all of equal importance. They are suggested as beginnings in a search for change. Some of them may not be useful or may not fit your particular local government. However, most can be adapted. Some may uncover issues that need more careful study than this format allows.

One other important thing to remember is that a community is not an isolated entity. Rather, it is part of a much larger social, legal, and political system. What's decided at the national, state, and even county levels can have awesome impacts upon a community's functioning. The following format directs attention only to the community itself. It will at least, however, give you a jumping-off point for beginning to understand your community:

(continued)

---

[3] Most of this format for analyzing a community or neighborhood was adapted from *Know Your Community* (1972), published by the League of Women Voters of the United States. Printed with permission from the League of Women Voters of the United States, Washington, D.C.

A. Community Characteristics

1. *Ethnic/Racial Configuration*

What are the major population characteristics (for example, what percentage is white, African American, Vietnamese, American Indian, or Hispanic)?
What are the principal ethnic and religious groups?
What is the age composition?
How do the population characteristics compare to state and national demographics?

2. *Economic Factors*

What are the principal economic characteristics of the community?
How are most of the people employed?
What are the major industries?
What other sources of wealth are there?
Have there been recent changes in the economic life of the community (for example, industries moving in or out of the area or having major expansions or cutbacks)?

3. *Unemployment*

What is the unemployment rate?
How does this rate compare with state and national rates?
What variables tend to characterize the unemployed population (that is, is it largely African-American, Hispanic, female, or within the eighteen to twenty-year-old age range)?
Have there been recent changes in this unemployment rate?
If so, to what can these changes be attributed?
Are there sections of the community where the rate is appreciably higher than the average?

4. *Income Levels*

What is the median or per capita income?
Is the average skewed because of large numbers of wealthy people?
Are there large numbers of poor people in the community?
How does the community's median income compare to state and national averages?

(continued)

5. *Housing Patterns*

What are the housing patterns within the community?

What percentage of residential property is high, moderate, or low cost?

What is the condition of the community's housing (for instance, mostly new, well-kept and maintained, or deteriorating)?

What pattern characterizes the range of rents in the community?

How available is moderate and low-cost housing?

Is the community dependent on a large metropolitan area for employment?

Is the community dependent on a large metropolitan area for the housing of those who work in this community?

B. Community Life

1. *Communication and Interaction*

How many newspapers are there?

If more than one, are they independently owned?

How many radio and television stations are there?

Are radio and/or television stations owned by newspapers?

Is community news carried on a regular basis in a metropolitan newspaper?

What are the principal out-of-town media influences?

How does one learn about local governmental activities, hearings, meetings, or cultural activities?

2. *Social Services*

What private social service agencies exist in the community?

Are there specific organized groups aimed at improving social services within the community?

Is there joint fundraising in the community such as that provided by United Way?

What types of fundraising exist in the community and why?

3. *Civic and Service Organizations*

What are the principal community-wide civic and service organizations?

Are there fraternal groups?

Are there labor organizations?

(continued)

Are there business organizations?

Are there cultural groups?

Do such groups work together on community-wide problems?

Are there coalitions among these groups on common interests?

Are such coalitions ad hoc groups or groups of longer standing?

Which groups are more likely to be aligned and on what kinds of issues?

Are there neighborhood groups?

If so, around what are they organized—cultural, school, political, or other interests?

C. Available Social Services

1. *Administration*

What governmental agencies (town, county, state, federal) are involved in operating the public welfare or social services in the community?

What employees are engaged in public welfare or social service activities?

How are these employees selected?

What qualifications are required?

What are these employees' salaries?

2. *Interagency Cooperation*

What cooperative programs, if any, exist between public welfare agencies and the juvenile court, probation officers, schools, day-care centers, nursing homes, public health services, and other agencies?

What cooperation, if any, exists between public and private social service agencies?

If so, what form of cooperation exists?

Is there regular exchange of information?

Is there any joint planning going on?

(continued)

3. *Noninstitutional Care*

What agency or agencies administer services for children who are orphaned or who have been abandoned?

Are foster homes used?

What is the rate of pay to foster homes?

How are such foster homes chosen?

How are such homes supervised?

What money is available for families and/or children in poverty?

What General Assistance is available?

What is the average amount available for each child?

What is the caseload per income maintenance and social service workers?

Are there efforts being made to help parents find jobs?

If so, what kinds of efforts?

Are there adequate day care centers?

4. *Other Public Assistance Programs*

What programs are there for blind and deaf persons?

What programs are there for permanently disabled persons?

What programs are there for partially disabled, elderly persons who don't qualify for social security?

What other assistance programs exist (for example, temporary assistance, special and corrective needs, exceptional needs such as bus fares and help during emergencies, employment services, legal services, or others)?

What money is available for such assistance?

From what sources is it available?

How do individuals apply for such assistance?

How is information about such special assistance made available to the people?

D. Summary

In one to two paragraphs, summarize your major perceptions about this community.

4. After about forty-five minutes your instructor will call you back for a large group discussion. Focus on the following questions:
   a. What did you learn about your campus's community from doing this exercise?
   b. What did you find out that you still don't know about the community?
   c. What information about communities can be most helpful in serving clients?

6 Planning in Generalist Practice

I. Introduction

II. Steps in the Planning Process

Figure 6.1: Planning in the Generalist Intervention Model (GIM)

A. Step 1: Work with Your Client(s)

B. Step 2: Prioritize Problems: Which Problem Should You Work On First?

1. Identify with client the range of problems that are most significant to the client
2. Restate each problem using explicit behavioral terms
3. Prioritize the problems in order of their importance to the client
4. Establish an initial agreement with the client regarding the problem you will attend to first

C. Step 3: Translate Problems into Needs

Figure 6.2: Examples of Related Needs Translated from Identified Problems

D. Step 4: Evaluate Levels of Intervention—Selecting a Strategy

1. Strengths

   Highlight 6.1: Potential Areas of Clients' Strengths

   a. Special interests and activities

   b. Family and friends

   c. Religion and values

d. Occupation and education

e. Reaction to professional services

f. Emotional and mental health

g. Physical condition

h. Support system

i. Other

2. Pros and cons

a. Macro strategy

b. Micro strategy

E. Step 5: Establish Goals: Five basic purposes for establishing goals:

1. Guarantees that workers and clients are in concurrence regarding what they want to pursue

2. Provide direction and continuity in the helping process

3. Aid in the identification, formulation, and evaluation of relevant strategies to proceed with the intervention

4. Help practitioners observe and appraise the progress being made

5. Serve as outcome criteria in evaluating the effectiveness of specific interventions

F. Step 6: Specify Objectives

1. Writing clear objectives

2. Objectives should be measurable

3. Sometimes goals and objectives are confusing

a. Objective should always be clear

b. Goal is often too complex to be measured

4. Setting objectives in micro practice

a. Establishing objectives

1) Objectivity

2) Clarity

3) Completeness

b. Ideal objectives can be measured

1) Performance

2) Conditions

3) Standard or level of performance

Highlight 6.2: Using the Concepts of Performance, Conditions, and Standards to Establish Goals and Objectives with Clients

Highlight 6.3: Clarifying Vague Goals and Objectives

5. Assigning tasks as part of the objective-setting process

G. Step 7: Formalize a Contract

1. Four major components

a. Specify what will occur during the intervention process

b. Established in agreement with worker and client together

c. Generally contains four types of information

1) Goals

2) Methods

3) Timetables

4) Mutual obligations

d. Can be written, oral, or implied

2. The purpose of a contract

3. Make contacts with clients

4. The format of a contract

a. The written contract

1) Advantages

a) Clear, virtually indisputable record

b) Participants sign the contract

2) Disadvantages

a) Takes time to draw up

b) Legal questions can be raised

b. The verbal contract

1) Advantages

a) Can be done swiftly and easily

b) Can be helpful with resistant clients who refuse to sign a written document

2) Disadvantages

a) Forgetting the details is easy

c. Implicit contracts: Agreements that are implied or assumed but not actually articulated

5. What to include in intervention contracts

a. Identifying information

b. Specified objectives

c. Signatures

d. Dates

e. Formats vary

Figure 6.3: An Example of a Written Contract Format

f. Contracts often change over time

Figure 6.4: An Example of Progressively Changing Contracts

g. Preliminary contracts

III. Planning in Mezzo Practice

A. The Complexity of Setting Objectives in Mezzo Practice

B. Contracts in Mezzo Practice

IV. Planning in Macro Practice

A. An Approach to Program Planning

1. Work with the client

2. Prioritize problems

Highlight 6.4: Planning a Health Clinic

3. Translate problems into needs

a. Get data and information to clarify need

b. Specify other agencies already addressing the identified need

c. Talk to other professionals involved with clients

d. Ask community residents how they perceive the problem and need

e. Consider a more formal needs assessment

4. Evaluate the levels of intervention

5. Establish goals and specify objectives

a. Determine whether the need exists

b. Marshal support for program development

1) Action group

c. Allocate responsibilities to a board or advisory council

d. Describe the purpose of the proposed program

e. Formulate clear objectives

f. Implement a feasibility study

g. Solicit financial resources needed to initiate the program

h. Describe how program will provide services

i. Get the program started

j. Establish how service will be provided on an ongoing basis

6. Formalize a contract

V. Chapter Summary

EXPERIENTIAL EXERCISES AND SIMULATIONS

Four exercises in this chapter focus on various aspects of the planning process described by the Generalist Intervention Model. Exercise 1 addresses prioritizing problems, Exercise 2 deals with translating problems into needs, Exercise 3 provides practice in clarifying vague objectives, and Exercise 4 concerns making a contract.

Exercise 1: Prioritizing Problems

A. Brief description:
Pairs will take turns helping each other prioritize an array of personal problems.

B. Objectives:
You will be able to:
1. Identify a variety of problems.
2. Prioritize these problems in terms of the order in which they will be addressed.

C. Procedure:
1. Before beginning this exercise, review the material in the text on the steps in the planning process. The planning process is summarized in the accompanying diagram.
2. Take a sheet of scratch paper and vertically list the letters *a* through *e*. Beside each letter, cite a problem you are currently having. Problems may range from the very broad (for example, not having any money or being depressed) to the very specific (for instance, setting up two different dates at the same time next Thursday night or forgetting to send your mother a birthday card). Do *not* list problems which you don't care to share (for example, you think you're pregnant). You will be asked to share the list of problems with your partner.
3. Break up into pairs. Take turns playing the worker and the client. First, the worker asks the client about his or her problems for approximately fifteen minutes. The worker should:
   a. Identify with the client the range of problems which are most significant to the client. (Problems should be included only when the client recognizes their significance, they can be clearly defined, and there is some possibility of finding a solution.)
   b. Restate each problem using "explicit behavioral terms" (Reid & Epstein, 1972, pp. 58-59).
   c. Prioritize the problems in order of their importance to the client.
4. After fifteen minutes, reverse roles and do the same thing.
5. Return to the class for a full class discussion which addresses the following questions and issues:
   a. How difficult was it to identify problems? Explain.
   b. How difficult was it to use "explicit behavioral terms"? Explain.
   c. How difficult was it to prioritize the array of problems? Explain.
   d. What problems tended to take highest priority (for example, the most serious, the simplest, or the easiest to solve)?
   e. How similar do you think this exercise is to prioritizing problems with real clients?

PLANNING IN THE GENERALIST INTERVENTION MODEL

FOUNDATION FOR GENERALIST PRACTICE

Knowledge *Skills* *Values*

↓

ENGAGEMENT

↓

ASSESSMENT

↓

PLANNING

STEP 1: **Work with the client.**

STEP 2: **Prioritize problems.** →

PROBLEM
1.
2.
3. etc.

STEP 3: **Translate problems into needs.** →

Problem	→	*Need*
1.	→	1.
2.	→	2.
3.	→	3. etc.

STEP 4: **Evaluate levels of intervention for each need.**

NEED #1: ______________ etc.

a. Identify Alternatives:	b. Propose Solutions	c. Evaluate: *Pros*	*Cons*	*Client Strengths*
MICRO				
MEZZO				
MACRO				

STEP 5: **Establish primary goals.**

STEP 6: **Specify objectives.**

	Who?	Will do what?	By when?	How will you measure success?
1.				
2.				
3.				

STEP 7: **Formalize a contract.**

Exercise 2: Translating Problems into Needs

A. Brief description:
You will be asked to translate a variety of problems into specific needs, after which the entire class discusses the activity.

B. Objectives:
You will be able to:
1. Demonstrate how a variety of problems can be translated into needs.
2. Explore the usefulness of this process regarding getting clients needed resources.

C. Procedure:
1. Review the material in the text concerning translating problems into needs.
2. By yourself, translate the following problems into needs:

Problem	Need(s)
1) Truancy	increase school appearances; stop making excuses.
2) Children don't listen	parent skills + discipline skills
3) Spouses are unable to communicate	marraige/individual counseling
4) No resources for paying the rent	explore agencies + expenses
5) Infertility	explore other alternatives
6) Wife is battered almost daily	
7) Sexual harassment at work	make awareness @ work
8) Being HIV positive	coping with HIV, support groups
9) Severe developmental disability	learn more about disability + why
10) Unwanted pregnancy	safe sex; sexual ed courses
11) Racial discrimination at work	teaching about other cultures
12) Rheumatoid arthritis	seeking information about coping with treatment.
13) Runaway adolescent son	
14) Cocaine addiction	make aware of treatment alts
15) Divorced spouse not paying support	
16) Violent teen gang in neighborhood	
17) Received drunk driving ticket	will not drink + drive
18) "Stuck" in minimum wage job	

3. After about ten minutes, join the class for a discussion concerning results. Review the problems one by one and discuss the respective needs involved. Afterwards, address the following questions:
   a. Which problems were the most difficult to translate into needs? What were the reasons for this?
   b. Which problems needed further clarification and why?
   c. How do needs provide clues for what services might be useful?

Exercise 3: Clarifying Vague Objectives

A. Brief description:
Via class discussion, address a series of vague objective statements, explore the reasons for their vagueness, and propose improved restatement of the objectives.

B. Objectives:
You will be able to:
1. Evaluate a number of value objective statements.
2. Explain the reasons why they are vague.
3. Propose improved objective statements using the performance/conditions/standards format.

C. Procedure:
1. Review the material in the text concerning establishing primary goals and specifying objectives.
2. In a class discussion, address the vague objective statements given below, one by one. Discuss the reasons why each statement is vague and establish improved objective statements. Use the performance/conditions/standards formula discussed in the text to formulate new objectives. Finally, clearly identify what portions of the new objectives reflect performance, conditions, and standards.

Vague Objective Statement	**Reasons for Vagueness**	**Improved Restatement: Performance/Conditions/Standards**
1. Promote emotional well-being	______________	______________________
2. Increase self-awareness	______________	______________________
3. Find adequate housing	______________	______________________
4. Facilitate adequate functioning	______________	______________________
5. Accept physical disability	______________	______________________
6. Dress appropriately	______________	______________________
7. Increase motivation	______________	______________________
8. Show interest	______________	______________________
9. Respond appropriately	______________	______________________
10. Improve self-concept	______________	______________________

(continued)

11. Develop a relationship	______________	________________________
12. Decrease hostile attitude	______________	________________________

Exercise 4: Making a Contract

A. Brief description:
Volunteers are asked to role play a family and worker. The worker then develops a contract specifying an initial intervention plan.

B. Objectives:
You will be able to:
1. Examine the contracting process.
2. Assess the specificity of objectives established in the contracting process.
3. Analyze the usefulness of contracting in the planning and intervention process.

C. Procedure:
1. Review the material in the text on formalizing a contract.
2. In preparation for a role play, read about the following characters:

Role Play Characters

Lucinda, sixteen, is referred to the Oconomowoc County Social Services Department by a local hospital. She just delivered Rosanna there two days ago and doesn't know what to do or where to go. Her parents, Frannie and Darryl, refuse to let her come home. They insist that she give the baby up for adoption. Lucinda adamantly refuses. Lucinda, a high school junior, is a C+ student. She has never presented her parents with major behavioral problems before her pregnancy. Gavin, seventeen, Rosanna's father, wants nothing to do with the situation and has not been in contact with Lucinda for five months.

Frannie, thirty-eight, Lucinda's mother, is distraught by her daughter's "sinful" behavior. She doesn't want Lucinda to "ruin her life" by giving up her childhood to be a mother herself. She feels that if she refuses to let Lucinda come home, she will force her daughter to give the baby up for adoption because she lacks other options. Frannie does not want "to start all over again" and help Lucinda with the many parenting tasks Frannie knows are involved. Frannie is very outspoken about her feelings.

Darryl, forty-four, Lucinda's father, agrees with Frannie, although less adamantly. On the one hand, he wants Lucinda to give Rosanna up. On the other, he loves his daughter dearly and worries both about what she will do now and about how she will feel in the future about losing

(continued)

Rosanna. However, he tends to be cowed by Frannie's strong will and volatile temperament. Darryl finds it much easier to agree with Frannie than to fight her, especially on major issues such as this.

The Worker, Ms. DeWitt, is an intake worker at the Oconomowoc County Department of Social Services. Her job is to work with initial referrals and establish beginning plans of action. Ms. DeWitt has read the initial referral information and has spoken with all three family members on the phone. This is her first face-to-face meeting with them. She needs to help Lucinda, Frannie, and Darryl come to some agreement and establish an initial contract regarding what they will do about Rosanna. She feels that foster placement is a viable temporary solution until the family can come to a decision concerning Rosanna's permanent placement. Rosanna remains temporarily at the hospital.

3. Volunteers are needed to play the various roles. They should assume places in the front of the class where other class members can easily see them. The worker's task is to establish an initial contract with the family following the "Contract for Intervention Plan" cited below. Note that the number of objectives can vary. That is, there don't have to be exactly five. The role play should last no longer than twenty minutes.

Contract for Intervention Plan

Client Name: ______________________________

I. Brief description of the problem:

II. Primary goals:

III. We, the undersigned, agree to the objectives in the following plan:

A. ______________________________

B. ______________________________

C. ______________________________

D. ______________________________

E. ______________________________

______________________________ ______________________________

______________________________ (Signature of Worker)

____

(Signature[s] of Client[s]

______________________________ ______________________________

(Date) (Date)

4. The Class should observe the role play until a contract is established or twenty minutes have passed (whichever comes first). The instructor should record on the blackboard the contract as it has been developed so that it's easier to discuss, even if the contract has not yet been completed. Discussion will focus on the following questions and issues:
   a. Summarize what occurred during the role play.
   b. What difficulties did the worker encounter?
   c. To what extent are the objectives clearly stated?
   d. What did you learn from the role play that you might be able to apply to contracting with your own clients in practice?

7 Implementation Applications

I. Introduction

Figure 7.1: Implementation in the Generalist Intervention Model

II. Child Maltreatment and Protective Services

A. Child Maltreatment

Highlight 7.1: A Profile of Child Maltreatment

1. Definitions and indicators

   a. Physical abuse

      1) Bruises

      2) Lacerations

      3) Fractures

      4) Burns

      5) Head injuries

      6) Internal injuries

   b. Behavioral response

      1) Overly compliant, passive

      2) Extremely aggressive, demanding, rageful

      3) Role reversal or extremely dependent

      4) Lags in development

   c. Neglect

      1) Deprivation of necessities

      2) Inadequate supervision

3) Emotional neglect

4) Sexual abuse

2. Incidence of child maltreatment

3. A profile of victims

4. Characteristics of abusers

a. Low self-esteem

b. Social isolation

c. Own emotional needs interfere with child care

d. Inability to nurture

e. Marital relationship problems

f. Extreme external stress

g. Inability to form loving attachment to newborn

h. Alcohol or other drug abuse

B. Family Preservation Philosophy

1. Holder and Carey's philosophical perspective

a. Problem seen as a social issue

b. Condemning and punishing parents who maltreat their children does no good

c. Concentrate only on working constructively with the families

e. Coordinate intervention efforts with other professionals

f. Most maltreating child caretakers can improve their conduct with support and assistance

g. Keep maltreated children within their own families if at all possible

h. Clients should always be integrally involved in the intervention

C. The Generalist Intervention Model: Engagement

D. The Generalist Intervention Model: Assessment

1. Interview and observe the child and family for indicators of mental health or clinical problems that suggest child maltreatment

2. Determine the degree of risk and the need to further involve the family with social services or law enforcement

a. Risk assessment

1) Maltreatment force

a) Type and severity of maltreatment

2) Child force

a) Maltreated child's personal characteristics

3) Parent force

a) Characteristics of the parents

b) Parents' child management skills

c) Parents' own upbringing and past

4) Family force

a) What variables characterize the family in terms of demographics

b) How can family function, interact, and communicate

c) What support and nurturance does the family receive from the surrounding social environment

5) Intervention force

6) Assessing the forces of risk

E. The Generalist Intervention Model: Planning

1. Self-sufficiency
2. Communication skills
3. Parenting knowledge
4. Stress management
5. Impulse control
6. Problem-solving skills
7. Interactive nurturing
8. Resource enhancement

F. The Generalist Intervention Model: Implementation

G. The Generalist Intervention Model: Evaluation, Termination, and Follow-Up

H. Child Maltreatment and Mezzo Practice

I. Child Maltreatment and Macro Practice: Five areas for improvement at the macro level

1. Focus on providing services aimed at prevention

2. More supportive system geared toward improving resources and services for families in general
3. More resources directed at treatment instead of case finding
4. Focus on treatment outcomes and improvement rather than on treatment process
5. Locate and develop more community and neighborhood supports

Highlight 7.2: Generalist Practice, Empowerment, and the Elderly

a. Micro practice
b. Mezzo practice
c. Macro practice

III. Crisis Intervention

A. Helps people learn to cope with or adjust to extreme external pressures

Highlight 7.3: An Example of Crisis Intervention in Micro Practice

a. Helping people cope with grief and loss
   1) Encourage to talk
   2) Negative feelings may surface

B. The Crisis Process

C. Major Concepts in Crisis Intervention

1. Primary goal is to help the client return to pre-crisis level of functioning
2. Relatively short term
3. Specific, observable difficulties become the target

4. Crisis intervention strategies generally work better than other approaches when dealing with crises

5. Practitioner in crisis intervention assumes a more active role than that assumed in other approaches to generalist practice

D. Steps in Crisis Intervention

1. Step 1: Assessment

   a. Determine why the person called or came to you that day

   b. How does your client view the crisis situation and precipitating event

   c. Does your client have access to support from others

   d. What is your client's history in solving similar problems

   e. To what extent is your client either suicidal or homicidal

2. Step 2: Planning

   a. Evaluate the extent the crisis has interfered with client's ability to function

   b. Review potential alternatives, evaluate pros and cons, and determine course of action

3. Step 3: Implementation

   a. Help the individual gain an intellectual understanding of the crisis

   b. Help the individual bring into the open present feeling to which she or he may not have access

   c. Explore coping mechanisms

d. Reopen the social world

4. Step 4: Anticipatory planning

a. Evaluation

b. Termination

c. Follow-up

E. Crisis Intervention at the Mezzo Level

F. Crisis Intervention at the Macro Level

1. Crisis intervention in most situations requires a multidisciplinary approach

IV. Alcohol and Other Drug Abuse (AODA)

A. Definitions

Highlight 7.4: Definitions of AODA Terms

1. Alcohol

2. Drugs

3. Substance

4. Intoxication

5. Abuse

6. Dependence

a. Tolerance

b. Withdrawal

B. The Alcoholic Person

1. Definitions:

a. They are consciously aware they are alcoholics, even if they don't admit it to others

b. They no longer can govern their drinking

c. They cannot stop drinking for any significant period of time

2. Four progressive phases of alcoholism

   a. Prealcoholic

      1) Drinking to reduce anxiety or stress

   b. Prodomal

      1) Increased loss of control

      2) Blackouts occur

      3) Once an individual starts drinking, cannot stop

   c. Crucial

      1) Greater loss of control

      2) Drinks more and more frequently

   d. Chronic

      1) Begins morning drinking and feels need to drink every four or five hours

      2) Physiologically dependent

      3) If a drink is not taken, nausea and shaking of hands may occur

      4) Alcohol removes these withdrawal effects

3. Typical defense mechanisms

a. Denial

b. Rationalization

c. Intellectualization

C. Alcoholism and Family Relationships

1. Norms or rules that sustain the drinking problem:

a. Dependent person's alcohol use becomes the most important thing in the family's life

b. Denial is paramount—alcohol is not the cause of the problem

c. Dependent person is really not responsible for his or her behavior—alcohol causes the behavior, always someone else to blame

d. No one should rock the boat, no matter what

e. Discussion of the family problem within or outside the family is forbidden

2. Seven phases families of alcoholics traverse:

a. Denial

b. Adjustment

c. Disorganization

d. Attempts to reorganize

e. Attempts to escape the problem

f. Reorganization of part of the family

g. Recovery and reorganization of the whole family

D. Your Role in Intervention with Alcoholics and Other Drug Abusers

1. Effective professional attitudes

a. An alcoholic is able to recuperate and improve

b. View alcoholism for what it is, namely, a disease that is out of the alcoholic's control

c. Be aware of telling symptoms that indicate an alcoholic problem

d. Remember that alcoholics have lost control

e. Confrontation is the most effective approach for dealing with alcoholics

f. The alcoholic must assume responsibility for his own behavior in order to get better

g. The entire family is part of the alcoholic problem

h. Know what resources are available

i. Avoid placing any labels on the alcoholic

E. Assessment of Dependence

F. Micro Practice Techniques for Implementation with AODA Dependent Clients

1. Interpretative therapy approach:

a. Alcoholics are excessively self-centered

b. Focus on the negative emotions the alcoholic is trying to flee

c. Alcoholism distorts one's perception of time

d. Focus on the distressed interpersonal relationship alcoholics suffer

2. Problems encountered in micro intervention with alcohol abusers:

   a. The problem of denial

   b. What if your client has a relapse?

      1) Treat the experience calmly, compassionately and briefly

      2) Treat the ordeal in as beneficial a light as possible

      3) Stress to the client that situations such as the one that led to the relapse should be shunned

      4) Help client manage stress that has led to drinking

      5) Help clients avoid relapses in the first place

   c. How do you get your client to trust you?

      1) Be straightforward and honest about your own abilities

      2) Do not be self-conscious and apologetic

      3) State what the treatment will involve

      4) Give direct feedback about their behavior

   d. What if your client arrives drunk?

      1) Docile clients should generally be calmly told to go home

2) Verbally assaultive clients: minimize the disruption and send client home safely

3) Physically defiant and threatening: minimize your own risks, do not try to counsel, someone else should call police

4) Consider whether to continue treatment

Highlight 7.5: Your Role as Referral Agent

e. Treatment options

1) Detoxification: Process of removing drugs or other harmful substances from the body

2) Outpatient services: Treatment at a health care facility without being admitted for overnight stays

3) Intensive outpatient rehabilitation: Clients may remain in own home but receive ten to thirty hours of rehabilitative services each week

4) Inpatient treatment: Clients remain in inpatient treatment all day and night

5) Specialty programs and tracts

6) Halfway house: Transitional residence for individuals who require some professional supervision but not full-time institutionalization

7) Personal care homes: People with extensive physiological damage caused by drug abuse may be admitted

8) Mutual self-help groups: Voluntary associations of nonprofessionals who share common needs or problems

9) Pharmacological adjuncts: Prescribed medications (e.g., Antabuse) to help begin the recovery process

G. Implementation at the Mezzo Level

1. Critical concepts for direct implementation with families

a. They must realize the extent of the problem

b. They need to learn about and evaluate their family dynamics

c. They should learn to confront the abuser

d. They need to learn about the progression of the disease

e. Abuser hits rock bottom, and may continue to probable death or struggle to help himself

H. Implementation at the Macro Level

1. Adequacy and effectiveness of treatment program

2. Accessibility of alcohol and other drugs to abusers

3. Prevention of drug abuse

Highlight 7.6: Integration of Policy and Practice: Managed Care Dilemmas

V. Chapter Summary

EXPERIENTIAL EXERCISES AND SIMULATIONS

This chapter focuses on the three major thrusts of chapter 7. Exercise 1 asks you to assess an alleged child maltreatment case according to the five major forces of risk discussed in the chapter. Exercise 2 describes a crisis intervention role play which the class evaluates. Exercise 3 provides four role plays of possible alcoholics where class members take turns asking questions and trying techniques.

Exercise 1: Risk Management

A. Brief description:
You are presented a case involving alleged child maltreatment, and are asked during a class discussion to assess the five forces of risk involved. Finally, you are asked to discuss what goals might be established for the family members and which specific service might be useful.

B. Objectives:
You will be able to:
1. Assess the five forces of risk present in a simulated case situation.
2. Formulate potential goals to work toward with the family.

C. Procedure:
1. Prior to doing this exercise, review the material in the text on risk management in protective services.
2. Assessment of the five forces of risk is an integral part of the risk management process. You will be asked to assess these forces (maltreatment, child, parent, family, and intervention) in the Ashton case situation.[1]

---

[1] The five forces of risk and suggestions for their evaluation are based on that described in the *Child at Risk Field System* developed by Wayne Holder, MSW, ACPS, and Michael Corey, MSW, ACPS, Action for Child Protection, Headquarters, 4724 Park Road, Suite C, Charlotte, NC 28209.

The Ashton Case[2]

The Presenting Problem

A concerned neighbor calls Milwaukee County Protective Services to report that Tiffany Ashton is abusing her eight-year-old daughter Dominique. A Protective Services worker named Ms. Stalwart reviews Ms. Ashton's records and visits the Ashton home to investigate the situation.

Ms. Stalwart finds Ms. Ashton extremely disoriented and depressed. Her sister recently died in a car accident due to her being drunk while driving. Apparently, this seriously affected Ms. Ashton's emotional stability. Ms. Stalwart takes Ms. Ashton to a Milwaukee Public Hospital and places Dominique in emergency foster care until Ms. Ashton's mental health improves.

Prior Agency History

Agency records indicate that nine months ago, Dominique's teacher had referred Dominique to Protective Services because she missed eight consecutive days of school without an excuse. The school could not reach Ms. Ashton by phone to find out what was wrong. Dominique's teacher indicated that Dominique's school performance has increasingly deteriorated over the past several months.

A Protective Services worker visited the home and found no evidence of habitation. A next-door neighbor indicated that Ms. Ashton and Dominique hadn't been around for several weeks. She said they had moved in with Ms. Ashton's boyfriend, Jagger, in a small flat a block away. The neighbor gave the worker the new address.

When the worker arrived at Jagger's apartment, Ms. Ashton appeared surprised but allowed her in to talk. The worker noted that Dominique had numerous bruises on her arms and legs. Ms. Ashton acknowledged that she had beaten Dominique with a stick three days earlier. Ms. Ashton continued that the beating resulted from Dominique starting a fire in her bedroom while Ms. Ashton and Jagger were out. Ms. Ashton said she had been so shocked that she beat Dominique to emphasize how dangerous firesetting was. Ms. Ashton and Jagger often left Dominique alone to fend for herself when they were gone.

(continued)

[2] This case is based loosely on a case study entitled "Case History #3: The Heller Family," in *Resource Materials: A Curriculum on Child Abuse and Neglect,* published by the U.S. Department of Health, Education, and Welfare, DHEW Publication No. (OHDS) 79-30221, 1979.

After a number of interviews, the Protective Services worker determined that the beating was a singular occurrence. Furthermore, Ms. Ashton regretted the beating deeply and expressed eagerness to cooperate with the worker. Ms. Ashton evidently did not understand that leaving an eight-year-old daughter alone for substantial periods of time was inappropriate and potentially dangerous. Ms. Ashton indicated that in the future she would make certain she found a babysitter before going out.

Four months later (and five months before Ms. Stalwart found her disoriented in her apartment), Ms. Ashton tried to kill herself by taking an overdose of sleeping pills. After she had spent several days in the hospital, her physician referred her to the local mental health center for treatment. However, she never followed through on this recommendation.

Two months later (and three months before Ms. Stalwart found her), Jagger beat Ms. Ashton up and threw her out of his apartment. She returned to her current apartment.

Prior Family History

Ms. Ashton's own personal history was turbulent. She was one of nine children raised in a poverty-stricken, multiproblem family. Her parents were alcoholics. They were divorced after her father was found guilty of committing incest with two of her sisters. Subsequently, Ms. Ashton and several of her siblings were removed from the home and placed in foster care for several years.

After becoming pregnant at age seventeen, she married Dominique's father, who deserted her shortly therafter. She contemplated giving Dominique up for adoption but decided against it. She never divorced Dominique's father because she still "really loves him." She became pregnant twice more with different boyfriends and gave both children up for adoption.

Since Dominique's birth, Ms. Ashton has been receiving public assistance. At Ms. Ashton's request, the County Department of Social Services enrolled her in three job training programs over the years. However, she soon dropped out of each, and so never neared completion. She experienced several bouts of depression for which she received medication. Until Dominique was three, Ms. Ashton lived with her own prior foster parents who provided Dominique with satisfactory care.

Dominique's History

Dominique achieved her developmental milestones within normal limits. Her childhood was healthy with the exception of common childhood diseases.

Dominique's teachers describe Dominique as a pleasant, likable child. However, she does poorly in school, especially in math and English. They indicate that Dominique has been seriously distressed by her mother's mental state, which has detracted from Dominique's school performance. *(continued)*

A recent report by a consulting psychologist indicates that, despite Ms. Ashton's emotional difficulties, she and Dominique have a "close, loving relationship." They care deeply for each other and, according to his recommendation, should not be permanently separated.

3. Your instructor will lead the class in a discussion regarding how the five forces (maltreatment, child, parent, family, and intervention) contribute to or diminish risk in the Ashton family. Your discussion should first focus on each force, briefly defined below. Address the questions relating to each force, note those areas where you need additional information, and arbitrarily evaluate the amount of risk you feel is present. Subsequently, evaluate the risk for each force as great, moderate, or small.

   It is beyond the scope of this workbook to undertake an extensive risk assessment as a worker would conduct in real life. This exercise is designed to help you focus on those variables contributing to risk in any particular family and make an arbitrary judgment about what should be done. In a real case situation, the assessment would assume much greater depth.

   a. *Maltreatment Force* involves the types and severity of maltreatment that are occurring in the home, and the conditions under which maltreatment usually occurs.
      1) Are the children being neglected, burned, beaten, or sexually molested?
      2) Is the abusive parent drunk, depressed, or explosive?
      3) Does the maltreatment occur randomly or only in times of crisis?
      4) What amount of risk does maltreatment force generate within the home—great, moderate, or small?

   b. *Child Force* involves the maltreated child's personal characteristics and the extent to which you as the worker perceive the child as being susceptible to maltreatment.
      1) Is Dominique extremely withdrawn, brashly aggressive, or exceptionally slow to respond?
      2) Is Dominique a very young child or physically disabled (which would make her exceptionally vulnerable)?
      3) What amount of risk does child force generate within the home—great, moderate, or small?

   c. *Parent Force* entails the characteristics of parents in the family, the parents' child management skills, the parents' own upbringing and past experiences, and the interactional patterns of the parents with others.

1) *Ms. Ashton's Characteristics:*
   a) How does Ms. Ashton feel about herself?
   b) Does she feel guilty after maltreatment occurs?
   c) How does she cope with external stresses?
2) *Ms. Ashton's Parenting Skills:*
   a) To what extent does Ms. Ashton rely on physical punishment to control Dominique?
   b) How responsive is Ms. Ashton to Dominique's wants and demands?
3) *Ms. Ashton's Own Upbringing:*
   a) How was Ms. Ashton treated by her own parents?
   b) Do they have a prison record or record of legal convictions?
   c) Do they have health difficulties?
4) *Ms. Ashton's Parents' Interactions:*
   a) How do Ms. Ashton's parents communicate with other people?
   b) Do they have friends or neighbors with whom they associate?
   c) To what extent are they isolated from others?

In summary, what amount of risk does parent force generate within the home—great, moderate, or small?

d. *Family Force* concerns family demographics, family functioning and communication, and the overall support and nurturance the family receives from the surrounding social environment.
1) *Family Demographics*:
   a) What variables characterize the family in terms of demographics?
   b) Are one or both parents involved?
   c) How many children are there?
   d) Is the family a blended stepfamily?
   e) What levels of education, job training, and work experience do the parents have?
   f) What is the family's income level?
   g) Is unemployment a problem?
   h) What are there housing conditions like?
2) *Family Function and Communication:*
   If the parents are married, how do they get along?
   a) How involved is Jagger or other boyfriends with Dominique?
   b) How do family members talk to each other?
   c) How would you describe the family's lifestyle?
   d) Is the family prone to crises?

3) *Environmental Supports*
   a) What relationships does the family have with extended family members?
   b) Does the family have access to adequate transportation?
   c) Is the family socially isolated?

In summary, what amount of risk does family force generate within the home—great, moderate, or small?

4. Now address the following questions:
   a. What do you feel is the overall amount of risk to Dominique in the Ashton home—great, moderate, or small?
   b. In a real treatment situation, what types of goals might you as a worker pursue? Consider the following (Holder & Cary, 1991):
      1) *Self-Sufficiency*
      Parents and families frequently need to enhance their ability to function independently. This dimension has to do with families being better able to fend for themselves and satisfy their own needs. Specific objectives often involve increasing self-esteem and confidence.
      2) *Communications Skills*
      Goals focusing on improved communication skills among family members are common. Members can be encouraged to identify and express their feelings openly and honestly. Listening skills can be enhanced. Family members' ability to understand each other's point of view can be improved.
      3) *Parenting Knowledge*
      Parents may not know how to handle and control children. They may have been brought up in emotionally deprived environments themselves. They may resort to force for controlling children's behavior because they've never been taught any other behavior management techniques. They can be taught not only to control, but to play with and enjoy their children.

      Additionally, parents may need knowledge about normal development. They need to know what to expect in terms of normal behavior at each age level. Appropriate expectations may reduce the frustrations parents feel when children don't behave the way the parents think they *should.*
      4) *Stress Management*
      Parents can be taught to better manage their stress levels. They can be taught to release their feelings more appropriately, instead of allowing emotional pressure to

build up and explode. Learning specific stress management techniques such as relaxation approaches can also help them cope with stress.

5) *Impulse Control*
Many parents in families at risk have poor impulse control. They are under tremendous stress. They often need to learn how to direct their energies in more fruitful ways than by violently lashing out at children.

6) *Problem-Solving Skills*
Parents in high-risk families may be so frustrated and stressed that they feel they have little control over their lives and their behavior. They can be taught how to analyze problems, translate these problems into needs, establish potential alternatives for meeting these needs, evaluate the pros and cons of alternatives, and, finally, select and pursue their most promising options.

7) *Interactive Nurturing*
Many times family members need to be taught how to express their positive feelings, on the one hand, and accept affection, on the other. They can be taught how to empathize with each other, verbalize their feelings, and, hence, reinforce their support and caring for each other.

8) *Resource Enhancement*
A primary means of increasing the strength of families at risk is to increase their resources. Adequate employment, income, housing, food, and clothing all contribute to a family's well-being.

Exercise 2: Crisis Intervention

A. Brief description:
Volunteers are asked to role play two social workers and members of a family experiencing a crisis. Social workers focus on the planning and intervention phases of the crisis intervention model.

B. Objectives:
You will be able to:
1. Identify the steps in crisis intervention.
2. Demonstrate the application of these steps to a crisis situation.
3. Evaluate the approaches used during a role play.

C. Procedure:
1. Before beginning this exercise, review the material in the text on crisis intervention.
2. Volunteers are needed to participate in a role play involving crisis intervention. Otherwise, your instructor will assign roles. The roles are as follows:

Role Play: Crisis Intervention

Social Work Role: Two social workers are intake workers in a crisis intervention unit of a community mental health center. Their job is to meet with people who phone for help because of a current crisis, assess the situation, and make the appropriate referrals. They have already gathered the following information about the clients.

The Situation: The workers are meeting with Farrah, Francine, and Felicity. Farrah's husband, Festus, was killed in a car accident five weeks earlier. Francine, sixteen, and Felicity, twelve, are Farrah's daughters. One other child, Fulbert, four, is not present at the interview.

Farrah, thirty-four, had been happily married to Festus for eighteen years. Having married right after high school, she has never worked outside the home. She loves her children very much and is very concerned about what will happen to them now.

Farrah is a quiet, pleasant, soft-spoken woman who is overwhelmed with grief and with the terror of being alone. She loved Festus dearly and had a very close relationship with him. He tended to make most of the family's decisions. Farrah had gone from being dependent on her parents to being dependent on Festus. She felt relatively comfortable and settled in that role.

Festus, thirty-eight, had been an assistant at the Morbid Misty Eye Mortuary for the past seventeen years. He had been earning $32,000 per year.

The family has a small home with only ten years remaining on the mortgage at 7½ percent interest. Although the family had never been wealthy, they had lived comfortably and adequately. Farrah was exceptionally good at managing the household finances. Now Farrah has the following major concerns:

1. Grief at the loss of her husband.
2. Fear of loneliness.
3. Financial worries—house payments, food, clothing, etc.
4. Worry about the children—both their emotional and physical needs.
5. What she will do.

Francine (nicknamed Foofy), sixteen, is an outgoing, friendly young woman who maintains a B+ average in school. She is fairly well adjusted in school, participates in a number of class activities (including cheerleading and chess club), and has many friends.

Francine is suffering from terrible grief at the loss of her father. She had a very good relationship with him and misses him very much.

(continued)

It seems things in her life have gone pretty well up until now. But now everything has fallen apart. She doesn't know what to do. She's worried about her mother and siblings. She doesn't know what will happen to the family. It seems her father was always the strong one who held things together. She can't even concentrate on her schoolwork much anymore. She'd like to help her mother, but just doesn't know what to do.

In summary, Francine has the following major concerns:

1. Grief at the loss of her father.
2. Questions about what her mother is going to do now.
3. Worry over her siblings and what will happen to them.
4. Worry about what will happen to her.

Felicity, twelve, is a pretty yet shy and withdrawn girl. She lacks self-confidence and generally has had difficulties in school, both with grades and with making friends.

She, too, is very upset by her father's death. She feels he was the only family member she could talk to.

Felicity feels that Francine, unlike herself, always seems to do well and have things come easily for her. Felicity resents this and often finds herself becoming angry at Francine. She feels guilty about these negative feelings toward her sister.

Felicity loves her mother but feels that her mother sides with Francine on most issues. Felicity especially resents how her mother tends to speak for her and answer questions addressed to her.

In summary, Felicity has the following major concerns:

1. Grief at the loss of her father.
2. Resentment towards her sister Francine for "being better at everything" than she is.
3. Resentment towards her mother Farrah for never listening to her opinion.
4. Low levels of self-confidence.
5. Lack of friends.

3. Volunteers should seat themselves in front of the class where they can be observed easily. Each volunteer should display an 8" x 5" note card with the client name marked boldly so that observers can better remember which volunteer is playing which role.
4. The workers should focus on the planning and intervention steps in the crisis intervention model presented in the text. Assessment, of course, is an ongoing process. The role play should continue for twenty to thirty minutes. Your instructor will indicate to the role players when it's time to stop.
5. During the role play, observers should take notes on the form shown below as they address the following questions:

Role Play Feedback Form

A. What do you think are particularly *good techniques* used by the social workers? How did the *clients react* to these techniques? (Please be specific.)

B. Do you see any weaknesses or areas in which improvement would be helpful? (Specific suggestions for how to improve are beneficial.)

C. Do you have any additional thoughts or comments?

5. After the role play, your instructor will lead a discussion which focuses on the following questions:
   a. What feedback did you note on your feedback forms? Strengths? Suggestions for improvement? Other comments?
   b. What did you feel were the critical points in the role play?
   c. To what extent did you feel the workers followed and applied the steps inherent in crisis intervention?
   d. How did the workers feel while doing the role play?
   e. How did the clients feel in reaction to what the workers said?

Exercise 3: What Do You Do with a Drunken Sailor (or an Alcoholic Client)?

A. Brief description:
Volunteers are asked to role play possible alcoholics. The remainder of the class then responds concerning assessment information, potential referral sources, and addressing the role player's denial.

B. Objectives:
You will be able to:
1. Recognize the symptoms of alcoholism.
2. Propose and evaluate potential referral sources.
3. Demonstrate some techniques used to address denial in alcoholics.

C. Procedure:
1. Before beginning this exercise, review the material on alcohol and other drug abuse presented in the text.
2. Volunteers are needed to play the various roles cited below. Your instructor will first read them to you.

Roles

Stephanie, twenty-one, is a college junior who majors in education and loves to "party." She has been known to label herself a "party animal." She goes out drinking almost every night (after some studying, of course). She drank occasionally at parties during high school and even got drunk a dozen or two times. When she first got to college, she limited herself to going out and "getting plastered" only on Friday and Saturday nights. However, as time passed, she's found herself wanting to go out every night.

She has fun, all right. But twice last month she found herself waking up in bed with some guy she didn't remember ever seeing before. Those guys were pretty "sleazy-looking," too. How embarrassing! Each time she surely got out of there in a hurry. She hopes she remembered to use condoms.

After all, she's doing okay in school. Sure, her grades have slumped a little bit. She's dropped from a B+ to a straight C average. But that's because the older she gets, the more difficult her courses get. For example, that stats course is pure misery. She often tells herself she's doing fine.

She's not crazy about the headaches she has most mornings. It takes her a while to get going. But she's only missed six or seven mornings of class since the semester started. She's doing okay. She surely isn't an alcoholic or anything like that.

The problem is that as she was driving from one bar to another the other night, a cop (who must've come out of the Twilight Zone because she surely didn't see him) busted her for drunk driving. Rats. What a bummer. What a fine. She also has to take a series of drug education courses. Crummy.

(continued)

Carlo, thirty-three, works on the line at Darley Havidson Motorcycle Manufacturing Company making "hogs" (a slang term used by motorcycle enthusiasts to refer to "awesome" cycle machines.) He married Blair nine years ago after he "knocked her up." They now have four children whom he frequently refers to as "ye olde wailing brats." Sometimes, he thinks it's too bad he doesn't like children very much.

He works second shift so he doesn't have to see too much of the family. Blair works first shift at George Webb's hamburger parlor. Carlo sometimes thinks that people who work there are required to have bad complexions and a hundred extra pounds of fat. That's Blair, all right.

Carlo's one joy in life is going down to Heck's Tavern and having a few "brewski's" after work. He and his cronies inevitably close it down and stagger home. Carlo even volunteers for overtime whenever possible so he won't miss weekend nights. Otherwise, he contents himself with a few twelve-packs and TV (football when in season).

In a vague way, Carlo thinks he's not very happy with his life. But he doesn't like to think about it too much. It's too depressing. The job's boring and he's never completely sure he won't get laid off. Yet, he can't afford to quit and start over somewhere else. Blair's constantly "bitchin'" about his drinking when he does see her. She says he slaps her around when he's drunk. Maybe, just a little, but not much. It's a good thing they work different shifts.

Day after day, week after week, he waits patiently for closing time when he can "belt down a few" and forget all his humdrum problems.

The problem is that last week that crazy town cop gave him a drunk driving ticket as he was trying to drive home. Carlo wasn't really drunk. He only had a few beers. How do you expect a guy to be able to relax, anyhow?

Viki, fifty-seven, is an executive for an accounting firm. She's been married to Alex, a sixty-year-old engineering consultant, for thirty-four years. Their three adult children live with their own families in various peripheries of the country.

Viki's job is extremely demanding. She usually works eleven-hour days, often including weekends. Alex's job is also demanding, so they don't see much of each other. They never were much for socializing, anyway. In the free time he does have, Alex keeps busy with fishing, reading, and doing projects around the house.

Although Viki often states that she loves her job, she typically comes home exhausted. Her high-level position makes her feel very important. She feels she needs to keep striving for greater and greater accomplishments in order to keep up with her very competitive colleagues.

(continued)

Upon entering the door as she gets home, Viki can't wait to mix her first very dry martini. Then she can't wait to mix her next one . . . and the next. Finally, after a couple of hours, she passes out on the couch watching television. Meanwhile, Alex goes to bed by himself. Viki will usually wake up at 2:00 or 3:00 a.m. and crawl into bed. A few hours later, her alarm sounds and she's soon off to work again.

Martinis help Viki relax. It's tough to "wind down" after a whirlwind day at the office. She's not an alcoholic, though. She only drinks to relax, and then only a few martinis.

The problem is, she had to attend a going-away party for one of her colleagues two weeks ago. She only had a couple of martinis. That cop must've been parked outside the bar where the party was held, just waiting for her to come out. Anyway, he gave her a ticket for drunk driving. How mortifying. And to think she usually only drinks a little at home.

Mortimer, sixteen, isn't into school very much. His parents are always on his back, so he does go. But they can't make him pay attention. He is passing. What do they want? He even got a C in shop last term.

Mortimer's got a part-time job, working after school at the local Sentry supermarket. It's not much of a job. It only pays minimum wage, but it does keep him in funny money.

Mortimer mostly likes to go out with his friends. They'll go to a game, watch TV, or "scope cherubs" (that is, look for gorgeous younger women who adore "older" men). Occasionally, he and his friends will really "get down and party heavy." Maybe every month or so, he'll really "tie one on." So what? He's just trying to have a little fun. He's only young once, right?

It worries him just a tad, however, how he can never remember what happened after a major party. He just wakes up the next morning with a major hangover to match. So what? It only happens once in a while. He's just having some fun. He doesn't *have* to drink. He just does it to have some fun with his friends.

The problem is that last Saturday morning, his dad entered his bedroom with the most somber expression on his face. Mortimer wondered how anybody could be beet red in anger and yet resemble a hard, cold stone statue like that. That's when his dad stated in a deathly, steel-like calm, icy voice, "How'd you annihilate the right front fender on the Lexus last night?"

"Oh, s _ _ _ _," Mortimer thought to himself. He didn't remember a thing.

3. Using the suggestions for working with alcoholics and other drug abusers presented in the text, the remainder of the class should take turns approaching each client about his or her behavior and situation. Role players should be addressed in turn, one at a time. The discussion for each

client should take about 10 minutes. Your instructor will tell you when it's time to talk to the next client.

Class members should ask questions and make comments targeting three aspects of the situation:

a. Assessment of whether each role player is an alcoholic.
b. Addressing the problem of denial.
c. Determining what resources, if any, may serve as appropriate referrals.

4. Following this discussion, your instructor will help you summarize your conclusions.

8 Evaluation, Termination, and Follow-Up in Generalist Practice

I. Introduction

Figure 8.1: Evaluation in the Generalist Intervention Model (GIM)

II. Evaluating Social Work Practice

A. Definition and Purposes of Evaluation

1. Evaluation: A process of assessing the success or worth of an undertaking

2. Micro level: Determine to what extent our work with a specific client was successful

3. Mezzo level: Determine if the treatment or educational group achieved its purposes

4. Macro level: Determine whether entire programs accomplished their purpose

   Highlight 8.1: Evaluating Community Programs

B. External Factors in Evaluation

1. Economic

2. Political

3. Consumer

C. Obstacles to Evaluation

1. Reasons evaluation has not been an ongoing concern for workers

   a. Leaves practitioner vulnerable

b. Workers often too busy

c. Many agencies have not emphasized its importance

d. Most social workers lacked training in use of evaluations

2. Two major thrusts of evaluations

a. Monitor the ongoing operation of an agency

b. Assess the outcomes of the program

D. The Evaluation Process

1. Key terms and ideas

a. Formative evaluation

1) Focus on the process of providing help instead of the end product of help-giving

2) Occurs while planned change process is occurring

3) PERT charts

4) Oriented toward the future

5) Course and instructor evaluations

b. Summative evaluations

1) Focus on whether or not the outcome we anticipated at the beginning of our planned change process has been achieved

2) Conducted after completion of process

3) Look backward

4) End-of-semester examinations

c. Baseline

1) Measures the frequency, intensity, or duration of a behavior

2) Should be based on several observations and over a period of time prior to intervention

d. Validity

1) Extent to which we are measuring what we think we are measuring

2) Types:

a) Face validity: Commonsense judgment about whether the measure actually reflects what it is supposed to measure

b) Concurrent validity: When scores on one instrument correlate well with scores on another instrument that is already considered valid

c) Predictive validity: When a measure can be used to predict future events, e.g., SAT test scores

e. Reliability: Extent to which an instrument measures the same phenomenon the same way each time it is used

1) Interrater reliability: High level of consistency among raters

2) Measure can be reliable but prove to not be valid

f. Data-gathering methods

1) Surveys or interviews

a) Structured (specific set of questions in a structured format)

b) Unstructured (open-ended questions in an informal discussion)

2) Observations

a) Direct (person-to-person)

b) Recorded

(1) Videotape

(2) Self-reports (subjective)

(a) Depression scales

(b) Assertiveness schedules

Highlight 8.2: Finding Valid and Reliable Instruments

3) Products: Achievement of a specific task or change in behavior

4) Observational measures: Rely on others to observe a change in the client's behavior

g. Independent and dependent variables

1) Independent variable: One of the factors thought to influence or cause a certain behavior, phenomenon, or reaction (the helping process itself)

2) Dependent variable: Outcome or end product of the helping process (outcome is dependent upon the helping efforts)

h. Generalizability: Ability of a set of results in one situation to fit another circumstance or instance

1) Substantial number of cases is necessary

2) Members of group must be representative

III. Evaluation Designs for Direct Practice

A. Single-Subject Designs

1. Aimed at determining whether or not an intervention was successful

Figure 8.2: Single-Subject (AB) Design

2. Steps in implementation:

a. Identify an easily measured goal

b. Baseline established showing frequency of the behavior prior to intervention (Phase A)

c. Record kept of frequency of behavior during and following intervention

3. B Design

a. Used when there is no opportunity to establish a baseline

Figure 8.3: B Design Without a Baseline

4. ABC Design

a. Phase A: Period prior to intervention

b. Phase B: When social worker begins to provide an intervention

c. Phase C: Additional treatment prescribed

Figure 8.4: ABC Design

6. ABAB Design

a. A: Baseline

b. B: Intervention runs its course and is discontinued

c. A: Based on the measurement level when the last intervention stopped

d. B: Intervention is begun again

Figure 8.5: ABAB Design

B. Additional Perspectives on Single-Subject Design

1. BAB Design

a. Not sufficient time to do a baseline

b. B: Provide counseling

c. A: Records are kept of occurrence

d. B: Additional treatment

Figure 8.6: BAB Design with Multiple Baselines

C. Goal-Attainment Scaling

1. Used when achievement of the goal is sufficiently important to be used as the primary outcome criterion

2. Focuses on desired state rather than a problem

3. Various steps toward achieving a goal can be measured

Figure 8.7: Goal-Attainment Scaling

Figure 8.8: Modified Goal-Attainment Scaling

D. Task-Achievement Scaling

1. Evaluating the degree to which an identified set of tasks has been accomplished

2. Typically a five-point scale is used

Figure 8.9: Task-Achieving Scaling

E. Client Satisfaction Questionnaires

Figure 8.10: A Client Satisfaction Questionnaire

1. Disadvantage: Potential for misuse

F. Target-Problem Scaling

1. Evaluating changes over time

Figure 8.11: Target-Problem Change Scale

IV. Evaluation Designs for Programs

A. Needs Assessments

1. Front-end analysis

2. May be used after program has been in operation to determine if unmet needs still exist

B. Evaluability Assessments

1. Designed primarily to answer the questions:

a. Can this program be evaluated?

b. Is the agency evaluation ready?

C. Process Analysis

1. Designed to evaluate the way interventions in an agency are carried out
2. Client-satisfaction questionnaires

D. Program Outcome Analysis

1. Designed to tell us whether or not a program is working

E. Program Monitoring

1. Designed to provide information to the agency on all aspects of its operation

V. Issues and Problems in Evaluation

A. Problems in Generalizability

1. Random sample: All elements in a population have an equal probability of being included in a sample
2. Stratified random sampling: Ensures some important subset or strata of a population is not accidentally left out of a typical random sample

B. Wrong Choices of Evaluation Tools

C. Failure to Involve Clients in the Evaluation Process

D. Staff Distrust of Evaluation

E. Evaluation Process Interferes with Service-Giving

F. Alternative Explanations for Program Outcomes

Highlight 8.3: Alternate Explanations for Outcomes

1. History: Any event that occurs prior to the end of an intervention
2. Maturation: Process of aging

3. Mortality: Loss that occurs when some of the people in the sample begin to drop out
4. Creaming: Tendency of some programs to take only the very best candidates for a program
5. Regression towards the mean: Tendency for extreme scores to move towards the mean over time
6. Reactance: Reaction or change of behavior that occurs simply because of a new situation or environment

G. Unanticipated Consequences

1. Side effects:
    a. Harmful to client and others
    b. Neutral in their impact
    c. Beneficial
2. Regressive effects

VI. Termination and Follow-Up

Figure 8.12: Planned Change Steps in the Generalist Intervention Model (GIM)

A. Ethical Practice and Critical Thinking About Termination

B. Terminating Professional Relationships

1. Tasks of termination
    a. Decide when to terminate
    b. Evaluate achievement of objective
    c. Maintain and continue progress
    d. Resolve emotional reactions of the worker and client

e. Make appropriate referrals

2. Planned terminations

3. Unplanned terminations

Highlight 8.4: Unplanned Terminations in Groups

4. Other points about termination

5. Reactions and feelings in terminations

a. Extent and range of emotional reactions

b. Amount of contact

c. Size and type of system

Figure 8.13: Factors Affecting Reactions to Termination

d. Mixed feelings

e. Worker reactions to termination

D. Helping Clients at Termination

1. Planning for termination

2. Addressing feelings about termination

Highlight 8.5: Termination Feelings of Family and Group Members

3. Summarizing progress

E. Stabilization of Change

1. Helping clients maintain and generalize changes

a. Help clients select relevant and appropriate situations to work on

b. Help clients build confidence in their own abilities

c. Use multiple situations and settings when helping members learn new behaviors

d. Use naturally occurring consequences rather than creating artificial ones

e. Extend treatment through use of follow-up sessions

f. Reduce setbacks in other environments

g. Help members confront future problems by teaching them a problem-solving process

2. Stabilizing change in small groups

a. Vary use of group activities

b. Ceremonies (graduations) help intensify the sense of ending and acknowledge progress of client

3. Stabilizing change in large systems

a. Routinize procedures and processes

b. Clarification of policies and procedures

c. Reduce the influence of the change agent

4. Addressing ongoing needs of clients

VII. Client Follow-Up

Highlight 8.6: Possible Tasks for the Worker at Follow-Up

1. Actively represent the consumer

2. Discuss problems

3. Straighten out difficulties

4. Prepare the consumer

A. Doing the Follow-Up

B. Overcoming Barriers to Follow-Up

VIII. Chapter Summary

EXPERIENTIAL EXERCISES AND SIMULATIONS

There are four exercises in this chapter, each intended to help illustrate a major idea appearing in chapter 8. The first three exercises involve evaluation of practice. The first asks you to select an appropriate evaluation design for assessing effectiveness of a small program. The second activity requires you to apply your knowledge of several key concepts described in chapter 8. The third exercise asks you to determine which of several alternative explanations might account for the apparent "success" of an intervention. The final exercise involves applying your knowledge both of feelings associated with termination and of how to respond to client comments or behaviors during the termination phase.

Exercise 1: Evaluation of Practice

A. Brief description:
Working as a task group member in a role-play, you will apply your knowledge concerning evaluation of practice to a case situation.

B. Objectives:
You will be able to:
1. Select an appropriate evaluation design for direct practice,
2. Identify data which will be needed for that evaluation design and the sources of that data.
3. Identify the program evaluation design which is most appropriate to a given case situation.

C. Procedure:
1. Review the four evaluation designs for direct practice discussed in the text. They are single-subject designs, task-achievement and goal-attainment scaling, and client satisfaction questionnaires. Also review the five types of evaluation designs for programs (needs assessments, evaluability assessments, process analysis, program outcome analysis, and program monitoring).
2. The instructor will assign students to task groups of four to six people. each group will participate in a role play. Identify one person to serve as recorder for each group.
3. Below is a case situation describing the need for evaluation within a social agency. Read the case carefully.

Case Situation: The Morningside Center

Marian Edwards is the coordinator of juvenile services for the Monringside Center, a small private agency which has a contract with the Department of Human Services. Under the terms of the contract, the Morningside Center provides after-school recreational and group activities for adolescent males and females. The Department of Human Services is requiring an evaluation component in all future contracts, and the Morningside Center's contract is up for renewal. Marian has been asked to design an evaluation mechanism which will help determine whether Morningside Center is achieving its purpose of giving adolescents a place to go so that they can stay out of trouble. Many of the adolescents in the Morningside area are at-risk for involvement in delinquent behavior. It is this behavior that the Department of Human Services is most interested in preventing. Marian is meeting with her staff to discuss the need to design an evaluation program. You are part of that staff for purposes of this exercise.

4. Assess the four evaluation designs to establish which one seems appropriate for use in this situation. Use the following format for your assessment:

Design	**Pros**	**Cons**
Single-subject design:		
Goal-attainment scaling:		
Task-achievement scaling:		

Client satisfaction questionnaire:

5. Select the design which seems most appropriate to this situation and list three reasons why this design is best.
   a. Most appropriate design: ____________________
   b. Reasons why this design is best:
      1) ____________________
      2) ____________________
      3) ____________________
6. Identify at least two types of information which might be gathered for use in this evaluation. Identify the sources or methods by which this information might be acquired.
   a. Types of information:
      1) ____________________
      2) ____________________
      3) ____________________
   b. Methods for gathering information:
      1) ____________________
      2) ____________________
7. Assume that the evaluation design you select has been in use for two years. Of the five types of evaluation designs for programs mentioned in the text (needs assessments, evaluability assessments, process analysis, program outcome analysis, and program monitoring), which is best suited to the task of determining whether the Morningside Center is effective?

   ____

   ____

   Why is it the most suited?

   ____

   ____
8. Record your responses to items 5 through 7 and report them back to the larger class at the direction of the instructor.
9. Your instructor will lead a class discussion focusing on the following questions:
   a. Why do social workers seem more interested in "doing" social work than in "evaluating" it?
   b. Why is evaluation of social work practice important? To whom is it important?

c. Does a funding body such as the Department of Human Services have a right to require an evaluation component in contracts they sign with other agencies? Why or why not?

Exercise 2: Key Concepts

A. Brief description:
You will test your knowledge of key concepts used in the evaluation of practice. You will be given a list of statements, some or all of which may be incorrect. Your task will be to distinguish between those which are incorrect and those which are correct. You are to work alone on this project.

B. Objectives:
You will be able to:
1. Identify key terms used in the evaluation of practice and connect them with their meanings.
2. Recognize when such terms are being used incorrectly or misinterpreted.

C. Procedure:
1. Review the section of Chapter 8 entitled Key Terms and Ideas.
2. Listed below are several statements regarding some of the key concepts described in Chapter 8. Read each of them carefully.
3. For each statement, use the space provided to answer the questions posed.

Key Concept Statements

a. Frank says an assertiveness program which has proven successful with six nonassertive clients can be utilized for *all* nonassertive clients. He states the success of one program can be *generalized* to *all* clients with the same problem. Is he right? Why or why not?

____
____
____

b. A paper-and-pencil questionnaire seems to accurately distinguish between clients who are depressed and those who are not. Clients with a score over 30 on the questionnaire are usually given both medication and counseling when they are seen by a psychiatrist. Would this suggest that the questionnaire is a *valid* measure of depression? Why or why not?

____
____
____

(continued)

c. Mary and John are arguing about the meaning of *dependent* and *independent variables*. John says that the interventions he is doing with a family constitute the *dependent variable* and the changes the parents have made, such as praising the children more and communicating feelings to one another, are the *independent variables*. Mary says John has the concepts backward. Who is right and why?

____
____
____

d. Alice has been using an at-home pregnancy test to determine if she is pregnant. The test has given different results on three occasions. Alice says the test does not seem *reliable*. Is she right? Why or why not?

____
____
____

e. At the conclusion of each group session, Ed, the social worker, asks the group members to give their opinions about how well the group functioned during the session. Ed commented to a colleague that he does this as one type of *formative evaluation*. Has Ed correctly described this type of evaluation?

____
____
____

Exercise 3: Alternative Outcome Explanations

A. Brief description:
You will be given three case situations involving clients. Following each you will need to identify a possible alternative explanation for the successful outcome of the case.

B. Objectives:
You will be able to:
1. Identify alternative explanations for outcomes in various case situations.
2. Recognize when apparent success of an intervention might be explained by factors unrelated to your intervention.

C. Procedure:
1. Read each of the following case situations.
2. Select an alternative explanation for the outcome which seems most probable given your knowledge of evaluation.

Case Situation #1

A group for twelve delinquent adolescents was begun ten weeks ago by the Juvenile Probation Department. The group was voluntary and involved regular sessions with a probation officer who asked the members to talk about their feelings. Six of the members dropped out along the way. Each of the six that remained evaluated the group experience very positively. Which of the following explanations might better explain the "successful" outcome.

a. History
b. Maturation
c. Mortality
d. Reactance

What is the reason for your answer?

Case Situation #2

Five very nonassertive adults joined a group to teach them to be more assertive. The group met for twelve weeks. Each person in the group was given an assertiveness test before joining and during the twelfth session. All showed more assertiveness on the last test. Other than an effective assertiveness training program, what might account for the change in their scores from the first session to the last?

a. Maturation
b. Regression toward the mean
c. Mortality
d. Creaming

What is the reason for your answer?

Case Situation #3

You see an advertisement for a new program which claims a high rate of success in treating anorexia (an eating disorder). The only people admitted to the program are those who have been through a battery of tests and interviews. All candidates are evaluated on their motivation to change, and only those with the highest motivation are admitted to the program. What might explain the very positive outcomes claimed by this program?

a. Maturation
b. History
c. Mortality
d. Creaming

What is the reason for your answer?

Exercise 4: Addressing Feelings About Termination

A. Brief description:
In this exercise, you will be considering the cases of three clients with whom separate social workers have been working for six months. In each case, the worker-client relationship has focused on helping the client get back on her feet after she left a physically abusive spouse and acquired a job to support herself.

B. Objectives:
You will be able to:
1. Recognize feeling expressions associated with termination;
2. Identify possible techniques useful in helping clients deal with termination.

C. Procedure:
1. Read each of the following excerpts from a worker-client interview.
2. For each vignette, select one worker response which appears to be the most appropriate and circle your choice.
3. Compare your answers with the class.

Vignette #1

Joan is meeting the worker for the last time. She appears a bit red-eyed near the end of the session as they finish their discussion about how much as happened in the past six months. Ann, the worker, is unsure of what might be going on in Joan's mind since they have talked about termination at previous meetings. Which of the following might be an appropriate response on Ann's part?

a. Let's not get too choked up now; you are doing fine.
b. You seem a little teary just now. What are you feeling?
c. You seem upset. Should we meet once more to talk about how things are going?

Vignette #2

Jan has just gotten a new job as a nurse's aide. She seems happy and expresses her glee to her social worker, Dorothy, at their last session together. What should Dorothy say?

a. I am so happy for you and delighted that you have found something that really interests you. You really look excited.
b. You are happy now but I worry about how you will get along after our sessions are over. This has been an important part of your life and I would think you might miss it. Many others have.
c. Let's talk about how you're feeling about the ending of our relationship. I feel a bit blue that we won't be seeing each other every week.

Vignette #3

Susan appears distraught and anxious at the beginning of the next-to-the-last session. She states that she really does not feel that she has made much progress in her work with Mark, and wonders aloud whether this has all been a waste of time. Now Mark is confused. What might he say?

a. You seem pretty upset today. I wonder what's going on.

b. We have accomplished a great deal together and I wonder how you can say we haven't made much progress.

c. Susan, something is troubling you today. I sense that you may be reacting to the ending of our sessions. A common reaction to termination is to be fearful of the future. People often question whether they've accomplished anything. Perhaps you are a bit angry with me. Do any of these strike a chord with you?

9 Understanding Families

I. **Introduction**

II. **Families and the Generalist Intervention Model**

III. **Family Assessment**

A. Assessing Family Communication

1. Verbal and nonverbal communication

a. Intent

b. Impact

Highlight 9.1: An Example of Conflict Between Verbal and Nonverbal Communication

2. Avenues of communication

a. Consensus: Extent to which the receiver accurately hears and understands the sender

b. Condemnation: Regular patterns of family members severely criticizing, blaming, negatively judging, or nagging other family members

c. Submission: Feeling so downtrodden, guilt-ridden, or incapable that you succumb to another's will

d. Intellectualization: Staging all communication within a strictly logical, rational realm

e. Indifference: Remaining unconcerned, not caring one way or another, and appearing detachedly aloof

B. Assessing Family Structure

1. The family as a system

a. Boundaries and subsystems

1) Boundaries: Invisible lines of demarcation that separate the family from outside nonfamily environment

2) Subsystem: Subordinate system (system within a system)

2. Family norms

a. Rules that specify what is considered proper behavior within the family group

Highlight 9.2: Family Norms Vary Drastically from One Family to Another

3. Family roles: Individually prescribed patterns of behavior reinforced by the expectations and norms of the family

4. Balance of power within the family system

5. Assessing intergenerational aspects of family systems

C. Assessing Life-Cycle Adjustments

D. Impacts of the Impinging Social Environment

1. Assessing a family's access to resources

Figure 9.1: Family Access to Basic Resources (FABR)

2. Difficulties in soliciting personal information

IV. **Family Conflicts, Problems, and Their Resolutions**

A. Partner Difficulties

Highlight 9.3: An Example of Communication Problems Within a Marriage

B. Parent-Child Relationship Difficulties

1. Parent Effectiveness Training (PET)

C. Personal Problems of Individual Family Members

D. External Environmental Stresses: The Impact of Social and Economic Forces

1. Brokering

V. **Variations in Family Structures**

A. Single-Parent Families

1. Single teenage parents

a. Preventing pregnancy

b. Help during pregnancy

c. Helping adolescent fathers

d. Helping mothers after the pregnancy

1) Positive parenting and child-management skills

2) Avoiding more pregnancies

3) Future life planning

2. Assessment and personal values

B. Remarriage and Stepfamilies

2. Unrealistic belief systems

3. Insiders versus outsiders

4. Power

   Highlight 9.4: An Example of Life Within a Stepfamily

5. Loyalty conflicts

6. Boundary problems

7. Discrepant life cycles

VI. Human Diversity and Family Assessment: Keys to Empowerment

A. Acculturation: Adaptation of language, identity, behavior patterns, and preferences to those of the host or majority society

B. Immigration History

C. School Adjustment

D. Employment

E. Male and Female Interactive Patterns

F. Role of Extended Family

VII. Chapter Summary

EXPERIENTIAL EXERCISES AND SIMULATIONS

The exercises in this chapter address various aspects of assessing and understanding families. Exercise 1 asks you to assess the roles in your own family. Exercises 2 and 3 employ an assessment instrument which specifies and clarifies a family's access to a wide range of resources. Exercise 4 provides a role play involving problem solving with a married couple. Finally, Exercise 5 asks you to propose policies which are supportive of positive family functioning.

Exercise 1: Family Roles

A. Brief description:
You will identify the roles in your own family, share this information in pairs, and relate this information about roles to families you are likely to encounter in practice.

B. Objectives:
You will be able to:
1. Identify a variety of family roles.
2. Discuss how family roles are important in practice with families.

C. Procedure:
1. Prior to the exercise, review the material in the text on family assessment skills, especially that concerning family roles.
2. Focus either on your family of origin or on your current family configuration. Take about ten minutes to write down answers to the questions below about family roles[1].

Family Roles

a. What specific roles does each family member occupy?

____

____

____

____

b. Do the various roles played work well together for the family's benefit?

____

____

____

____

c. Are any of the roles ambiguous, redundant, or left empty? Please explain.

____

____

____

____

d. Is there flexibility among family roles so that the family is better able to adjust to crisis situations? Please explain.

(continued)

---

[1] These questions are used when assessing families. See A.M. Holman, *Family Assessment: Tools for Understanding and Intervention* (Beverly Hills, CA: Sage, 1983), p. 30.

e. Do the family's roles conform with basic social norms? (For example, society does not condone a criminal role.)

____
____
____
____

f. Do the family's roles function to enhance the family's feelings of self-worth and well-being or detract from these feelings? Please explain.

____
____
____
____
____

3. Separate into pairs and discuss your answers to each question with your partner.
4. After about ten minutes your instructor will call you back to join a full class discussion addressing the following questions:
   a. What roles are most pronounced in your family?
   b. What value judgments did you find yourself making about your family's roles?
   c. What roles do you think are most pronounced in families generally?
   d. What roles do you think emphasize the uniqueness of your family?
   e. Can you think of a dysfunctional family you know?
   f. What, if any, problems regarding roles did the family members experience?
   g. What types of role problems do you think you will be most likely to confront in practice?

Exercise 2: Family Resources

A. Brief description:
You will be asked to complete a portion of a family resource assessment instrument and discuss the experience with the class.

B. Objectives:
You will be able to:
1. Assess the resources available to your own "family".
2. Relate this experience to real practice situations.
3. Recognize the variety of resources potentially available to families in need.

C. Procedure:

1. Before beginning the exercise, review the information provided in the text concerning assessing a family's access to resources.
2. Take about 10 minutes to fill out the form presented below, which is the first sections of "Family Access to Basic Resources (FABR)."[2] Before beginning, establish the boundaries of your family. Focus on your current family, your family of origin, or yourself if you are single. It doesn't matter which family group you decide is appropriate. The important thing is to have a specific family group in mind.

Family Access to Basic Resources (FABR)

Part 1—Monthly expenses for a family of this size and composition

Work expenses
- Transportation: $___
- Child care: ___
- Taxes: ___

Purchases for basic needs
- Decent housing: ___
- Utilities: ___
- Food: ___
- Clothing: ___
- Personal care: ___
- Recreation: ___

Health care
- Medical: ___
- Dental: ___
- Mental health: ___
  - Special (e.g., substance abuse): ___
- Education: ___
- Family & developmental (counseling) services: ___
- Procurement of resources/ services (e.g., transportation): ___

Monthly Total: $___

Part 2—Potential monthly family resources

Money income
- Wages (if parents' occupations are known, what are average monthly wages for these types of jobs?): $___
- Child support (if applicable): ___
- Income transfers (for those unemployed or not expected to work)
  - Unemployment insurance: ___
  - Worker's compensation: ___
  - Social Security: ___

(continued)

[2] Reprinted from Nancy R. Vosler, "Assessing Family Access to Basic Resources: An Essential Component of Social Work Practice," in *Social Work*, 35(5) (1990), pp. 436-37. Reprinted with permission of the author and of the National Association of Social Workers, Silver Spring, MD.

Supplemental Security Income (SSI):	___
Aid to Families with Dependent Children (AFDC)[3]:	___
Other (e.g., general relief, emergency assistance):	___
Credits, goods, and services (free or sliding scale):	
Housing	
Section 8:	___
Other housing assistance (e.g., public housing, shelter, hotel/motel):	___
Utilities assistance:	___
Food	
Food stamps:	___
Women's, Infants', and Children's Supplementary Food Program (WIC):	___
Food bank, food pantry, and other food assistance:	___
Monthly Total:	$___
Clothing: Access to used clothing store?	Yes ☐ No ☐
Personal care and recreation:	
Access to free recreational facilities?	Yes ☐ No ☐
Health care	
Medicare?	Yes ☐ No ☐
Medicaid?	Yes ☐ No ☐
Health clinic?	Yes ☐ No ☐
Dental clinic?	Yes ☐ No ☐
Mental health services?	Yes ☐ No ☐
Special services (e.g., drug abuse treatment)?	Yes ☐ No ☐
Education	
Public education?	Yes ☐ No ☐
Special education?	Yes ☐ No ☐
Tutoring?	Yes ☐ No ☐
General Equivalency Diploma (GED)?	Yes ☐ No ☐
Job Training?	Yes ☐ No ☐

(continued)

[3] AFDC was "a public assistance program . . . funded by the federal and state governments to provide financial aid for needy children who are deprived of parental support because of death, incapacitation, or absence" (Barker, 1995, p. 14). The Personal Responsibility Act (PRA) passed by Congress in August, 1996, abolished AFDC "which had provided support for poor children and their mothers since its inception at Title IV of the 1935 Social Security Act;" AFDC was replaced by "block grants for Temporary Assistance to Needy Families (TANF) which "put a cap on federal funds provided to the states" and allowed states greater discretion in benefit distribution (Abramovitz, 1997, pp. 311-312). The purpose of the FABR questionnaire is to determine resources regardless of their source. Therefore, you might replace the AFDC category with other new programs providing benefits to children and families.

Family and developmental (counseling) services

Family services?	Yes ☐ No ☐
Support groups?	Yes ☐ No ☐
Family life education?	Yes ☐ No ☐

Procurement

Transportation?	Yes ☐ No ☐

Part 3—Current Resources

Access to resources last month

Money income

Wages (use net pay; then subtract other work expenses from Part I including child care, transportation, etc.):	$___	Clothing:	$___
Child Support:	___	Personal care and health care:	___
Income transfers:	___	Education:	___
Credits, goods, & services:	___	Family & developmental services:	___
Housing:	___	Procurement:	___
Food:	___	Monthly Total:	___

3. For about ten minutes, address the following questions in a class discussion:
   a. How did it feel to fill out the FABR?
   b. To what extent was it uncomfortable to share such personal information?
   c. To what extent could you remember all of the detailed information requested?
   d. Were there resources mentioned on the form that you didn't know about or didn't understand? If so, which ones and why?
   e. How useful do you think the FABR might be in real worker/client practice situations?
   f. What did you learn from this experience?

Exercise 3: Clarifying Family Resources

A. Brief description:
After completing Exercise 2, you will divide into pairs to complete the worker/client portion of the FABR.

B. Objectives:

You will be able to:

1. Employ a portion of a family resources assessment instrument in a simulated situation.
2. Clarify and collect detailed resource information.

C. Procedure:

1. Before beginning the exercise, review the information provided in the text concerning assessing a family's access to resources.
2. Complete Exercise 2 above.
3. Divide into pairs. Arbitrarily determine who will be the "worker" (that is, the person who will do the assessment) and who will be the "client" (that is, the person providing information).
4. The worker should take about twenty minutes to complete the portion of the Family Access to Basic Resources (FABR) questionnaire provided below. This involves clarifying some of the information already gathered in Exercise 2.

Resource Stability[4]

How stable was each resource over the past year (very stable, somewhat stable, somewhat unstable, very unstable)? Discuss for each type of resource.

Wages: Overall access to wages through employment? Types of jobs available? Part-time or full-time? Wage levels? Benefits? How would/do you deal with child care or supervision of youth? Quality of child care? Do you have choices? How would/do you deal with an ill child? How would/do you get to and from work? What education and training are needed for good jobs? What education and training opportunities are available? Have you been laid off or terminated or experienced a plant closing? Number of times unemployed? Length of time unemployed?

Housing: Rent or own? Choice? Maintenance a problem? Are utilities adequate? Have you been put on a waiting list or been dropped from Section 8 or other housing assistance? Have you had to move or been evicted because the landlord converted to higher rents, condominiums, etc.? Have you experienced homelessness?

Clothing: Variety for different roles?

(continued)

[4] Reprinted from Nancy R. Vosler, "Assessing Family Access to Basic Resources: An Essential Component of Social Work Practice," in *Social Work* 35(5) (1990), pp. 436-37. Reprinted with permission of the author and of the National Association of Social Workers, Silver Spring, MD.

Personal care and recreation: What kinds of recreation? Individual? Family?

Health Care: High quality? Choice? Available in a crisis? Have you been dropped from health care coverage with an employer or from Medicaid? If so, why? Have you or another family member been put on a waiting list, for example, for medical or dental care, for counseling for a mental health problem, or for treatment for alcohol or drug abuse? If so, how long did the person have to wait for services?

Other comments and reflections:

5. Rejoin the class for a ten minute discussion focusing on the following questions and issues:
   a. For the worker, how difficult was it to clarify the resources?
   b. What areas, if any, did you have difficulty understanding?
   c. Did you find yourself making value judgments in any areas?
   d. For the client, how did it feel to participate in the interview process?
   e. What information, if any, did you feel the worker misunderstood or missed?
   f. How useful do you feel such a resource assessment instrument would be in real practice situations? Why or why not?
   g. To what extent do you feel such an instrument might give you clues to undertaking macro and mezzo interventions? What are your reasons?

Exercise 4: Problem Solving with Couples

A. Brief description:
Volunteers participate in a role play where a married couple comes to two social workers for help. The remainder of the class observes and gives feedback.

B. Objectives:
You will be able to:
1. Apply interviewing and problem-solving techniques to a family situation involving marital difficulties.
2. Examine the interaction of the persons playing the married couple.

C. Procedure:
1. Review the material in the text on family assessment skills and family conflicts.
2. Volunteers are needed to assume the following roles:

Role Play: Problem Solving with Couples

Social Work Role:
Two social workers do intake and provide some problem-solving counseling for Oshkosh County Social Services Department. The county is primarily rural so the workers assess a wide range of problems, provide help, and make referrals where appropriate.

Client Role:
Fred, twenty-seven, is a pleasantly attractive, slender person with an outgoing, likable personality. He works second shift in a donut factory, and has an annual salary of $22,000.

Client Role:
Ethel, twenty-five, is a nervous, intense person who frequently has a worried expression on her face. She refers to herself as being "very shy." She has a pretty face and is about twenty-five pounds overweight. Since before her marriage she has worked as a secretary for the phone company. She earns approximately $18,000 annually. She also appears basically likable and eager to please.

The Presenting Problem:
Fred and Ethel have been married for four years. They come to Social Services because they are experiencing "marital problems."

Fred says that the problem is that he and Ethel fight all the time when they're together. He says he loves his wife and is committed to making his marriage work. He does not believe in divorce for moral and religious reasons. He and Ethel both want to have a family in a few years. He says Ethel always nags him about going out for a few beers after work with the boys and about how he really doesn't love her. No matter how much he tells her he loves her, she doesn't seem to believe him.

Ethel says the problem is that Fred ignores her all the time. He doesn't seem very interested in talking to her or spending time with her. She says she loves him very much and is committed to making the marriage work. She does not believe in divorce for moral and religious reasons. She and Fred both want to have a family in a few years. Ethel says she's getting more and more depressed about their marital situation and lack of communication. She constantly criticizes herself and wonders what she's doing wrong.

3. Fred and Ethel also have hidden agendas which are recorded at the end of this chapter's exercise section. *Do not look at them at this time.* Only Fred and Ethel should read them before the role play. One intent of this exercise is for the workers to seek out information and identify problems. The hidden agendas will be shared later after the role play.
4. The role play will begin in the middle of the interview. It is assumed that the workers have already gathered the information cited above. Their task

now is to complete their assessment, prioritize problems, and make referrals as appropriate.

5. During the role play, observers should take notes as they address the following questions:

Feedback Form

A. What do you think are particularly *good techniques* used by the social workers? How did the *clients react* to these techniques? (Please be specific.)

B. Do you see any weaknesses or areas in which improvement would be helpful? (Specific suggestions for how to improve are beneficial.)

C. Do you have any additional thoughts or comments?

5. The role players should sit in the front of the room where other students can clearly observe them. The role play should last no longer than thirty minutes.
6. After thirty minutes, your instructor will stop the role play and read Fred and Ethel's hidden agendas described at the end of this chapter's Exercise section.

7. The class will then participate in a discussion addressing the following issues and questions:
   a. What feedback did you note on your forms? Strengths? Weaknesses? Other comments?
   b. How much of the clients' hidden agendas surfaced during the interview?
   c. To what extent were the issues and future plans clear by the end of the interview?
   d. To what extent do you think this role play might relate to the issues of real client couples?
   e. What did you learn from participating in or observing this role play?

Exercise 5: Policies Impact Families

A. Brief description:
You will break up into small groups and propose policies which would foster positive family environments.

B. Objectives:
You will be able to:
1. Evaluate several policy areas directly impacting families.
2. Propose improved policies conducive to positive family life.

C. Procedure:
1. Break down into groups of four to six persons.
2. For thirty minutes, discuss the policy questions listed below in six major policy areas impacting families. A volunteer should take notes so that your results can be shared later with the entire class. You should make specific suggestions when appropriate, and answer "yes" or "no" to closed-ended questions.

Policy Areas Impacting Families

a. *Employment*
1) What policies do you think would increase employment and decrease unemployment?
2) Should government subsidize industry in order to hire new workers or prevent laying off current workers?
3) Should taxes be levied on foreign imports?
4) Should the government expand old and set up new job training programs?
5) What would the costs of such policies be?
6) What can you do to help your clients gain adequate employment under such circumstances if few or no programs and policies exist to help you?

(continued)

b. *Direct provision of income or substitutes for income*

1) What do you do when your clients aren't eligible for enough cash and in-kind (for example, food stamps) income transfers to survive?
2) What do you do if policies neglect clients who are slowly starving to death?

c. *Health care* (Millions of poor underemployed and unemployed people in this country are not covered.)

1) What health care policies should this country adopt to cover your clients who are poor and not currently covered?
2) Who should pay for such programs?

d. *Homeless people*

1) What can you as a social worker do if there are no programs with policies to provide your clients temporary shelter, food, and longer-term housing?
2) What can you do if families are living literally on the streets?

e. *Day care* (Most women work. More specifically, most women with children work. Adequate day care for their children is often difficult to find. It's also expensive and the quality is highly variable.)

1) Should the federal, state, and/or local governments establish policies to provide resources for day care so that parents can work?
2) Are you and others willing to pay taxes to finance these services?
3) What if your client is a single parent who receives public assistance payments barely allowing her to subsist below the poverty level? When benefits cease and she is forced to seek employment outside of the home, what if she can't afford the available day care? What policy changes might help her?

f. *Child support maintenance* (Policies dictate how much support divorced fathers provide their children. [Of course, mothers may also be required to provide support to children living with their fathers; however, this occurs infrequently.] Policies also mandate how the receipt of that support is monitored.)

1) What if your single-parent, female client is not receiving the child support payments she needs to survive?
2) Do existing policies indicate that a portion of the father's salary can be garnisheed, that is, legally removed from his pay and sent to his family before he receives his paycheck?
3) Will policies mandate that this happens automatically, or must the mother seek legal counsel to advocate for her?
4) What happens if the father moves to another state?

(continued)

5) Will that state's policies allow the garnishment of wages?
6) What if your client, a single parent and mother of two, works for a minimum wage, can't afford adequate housing on that income, and desperately needs support payments to subsist?

3. After thirty minutes, your instructor will call you back into a full class discussion where you will share and address your group's findings.

HIDDEN AGENDAS FOR EXERCISE 4

Fred's Hidden Agenda

Fred has very high expectations for himself concerning being a good provider and husband. He gets very threatened both when Ethel criticizes him and when he feels that he's losing control of his marriage.

Fred's also afraid that Ethel's secretly drinking too much. Sometimes he smells liquor on her breath. Sometimes he finds her passed out. He's also found empty liquor bottles in the garbage. He hasn't said anything about this to her. He's afraid to confront her with it because he thinks it will move them closer to a divorce.

At this point, Fred doesn't know what to do, so he has withdrawn from Ethel. He tries to be pleasant to her but really doesn't talk to her very much. Sometimes to avoid her he goes out for a beer after work with his male friends at the factory.

Ethel's Hidden Agenda

Ethel is a very insecure person with a fairly poor self-concept. She is an expert on what is wrong with herself and sometimes wonders what Fred really sees in her. Her weight also bothers her. Sometimes she just can't stand it anymore and withdraws into drinking. She knows this is wrong and feels very guilty about it. She's drinking just about every day now. She doesn't want Fred to find out and doesn't want to talk about it.

Ethel's really afraid that Fred is turning to other women. There are several attractive women at the donut factory that she's met at parties and that Fred has casually mentioned in the past. She's terrified of losing Fred. Fred works six second-shift days a week and goes out almost every night "with the boys." Ethel thinks he's secretly having an affair. This hurts Ethel terribly. However, she is following her typical pattern of avoidance and has avoided mentioning this to Fred. Frustration has built up and she finds herself nagging and yelling at him a lot for little things.

10 Working with Families

I. **Introduction**

II. **Generalist Practice with Families**

III. **Family Treatment and the Planned Change Process**

IV. **Strategizing for Family Intervention: Do You Always Have to See the Entire Family?**

- A. Advantages:
    1. Observing entire family in interaction can give great insight to understanding its dynamics
    2. Better able to assess and understand the problem from the perspective of all family members
    3. Opportunity to see communication patterns
- B. Not Always Possible or Appropriate

V. **Engagement, Assessment, and Planning with Families**

- A. Phase 1: Alleviate or At Least Minimize Early Apprehension
- B. Phase 2: Ask Family Members to Explain What Is Wrong
- C. Phase 3: Establish Agreement about What Is Wrong
    1. Techniques for engineering a problem consensus:
        - a. Focus on a problem that family will agree on
        - b. Recast problems from individual terms to problems of interactions of the whole family

c. Help family articulate what they are not able to express

d. Present problems to the family in the order you consider them important

1) Ask family members to rank them

2) Compare and contrast the results

e. Prevent family members making an individual a scapegoat

D. Phase 4: Concentrate on How Family Members Relate to Each Other

1. Direct questions to members that further explore the problems

Highlight 10.1: Four Ways of Exploring a Target Problem

a. The situation

b. Exploration of the problem

1) How long has the problem existed?

2) How intense has the problem become in the last two weeks?

3) What have family members done to solve the problem in the past?

4) What barriers have been operating both inside and outside the family that have prevented the problem's solution until now?

c. Summary

d. So what happens?

2. Instruct family members to talk to each other about the problem

3. Instruct only two family members to talk about how to solve the problem with each other

E. Phase 5: Establish Commitment to a Plan of Action

VI. Implementation of Family Intervention

A. Reframing: Helping family members view a problem or an issue with a different outlook or understand it in a new way

B. Teaching Families Problem Solving Techniques

C. Teaching Child Management Methods

1. Positive reinforcement: A procedure or consequence that increases the frequency of the behavior immediately preceding it

2. Negative reinforcement: The removal of a negative or aversive event or consequence that serves to increase the frequency of a particular behavior

3. Punishment: The presentation of an aversive event or the removal of a positive event that results in the decreased frequency of a particular behavior

4. Modeling: The learning of behavior by observing another individual engage in that behavior

D. Offering Families Support

E. Role Playing: Having a person assume a different role or part than she or he normally would

F. Videotaping

G. Homework Assignments: Tasks given to clients to be completed at home

VII. Evaluation, Termination, and Follow-Up with Families

VIII. Family Issues and Services

A. Multiproblem Families

1. Do not get overwhelmed yourself
2. Follow the planned change process as you would with any other situation
3. Partialize and prioritize the problems involved
4. Determine which, if any, problems you can work on yourself
5. Identify and use community resources

B. Family Preservation

1. Major themes in family preservation
    a. Crisis orientation
    b. Focus on family
    c. Home-based services
    d. Time limits
    e. Limited, focused objectives
    f. Intensive, comprehensive services
    g. Emphasis on education and skill building
    h. Coordination
    i. Flexibility
    j. Accessibility
    k. Accountability
2. Family preservation and planned change

a. Engagement

b. Assessment

c. Planning: Suggestions for goal formulation:

1) Client must feel goals are significant

2) Goals should emphasize social interaction both among family members and between them and others in the social environment

3) Goals should be small, simple, and realistically achievable

4) Goals should be viewed in terms of what can be done positively instead of focusing on problems

5) Emphasis that goals are difficult to achieve

d. Implementation

e. Evaluation

f. Termination

g. Follow-Up

C. Diversity and Families

1. Lesbian and gay families

a. Homophobia: Obsessive hostility and fear toward homosexuals

Highlight 10.2: Confronting Homophobia

b. Lesbians and gay men as parents

c. Coming out to children

1) Parents need to be comfortable with the fact that they are gay or lesbian

2) Parents need to plan exactly what to tell their children about sexual orientation

3) Timing

d. Lesbian and gay parents and child custody issues

e. Social and economic oppression of lesbian and gay people

2. Working with African American Families

a. The many strengths of African American families

Highlight 10.3: The Impacts of History and Oppression on African American Families

a) History of slavery

b) Ongoing oppression

1) Tend to have strong kinship bonds among a variety of households

2) Flexibility of family roles

3) Dedication to religious values and serious involvement in their churches

b. Social work practice with African American families

1) Engage the client family

2) Assess the family in past and present

3) Set mutual goals

4) Identify the target system for change

D. The Current Status of Family Services

E. Macro Practice with Families: Promoting Social and Economic Justice

Highlight 10.4: Families, Macro Practice, and the Integration of Policy and Practice

1. Employment
2. Direct provision of income or substitutes for income
3. Health care
4. Homeless people
5. Day care
6. Child support and maintenance

IX. Chapter Summary

EXPERIENTIAL EXERCISES AND SIMULATIONS

Three detailed role plays are described for exercises in this chapter. They include a nontraditional family, a lesbian parent who wants to come out to her children, and a multiproblem family. Exercise 1 targets beginning techniques with families for the focus of the role play; Exercise 2 explores approaches for coming out to children; and Exercise 3 discusses specific techniques for working with multiproblem families. Exercise 4 structures the application of reframing or role-playing to one of the role-plays described earlier.

Exercise 1: Beginning with Families

A. Brief description:
Volunteers role play a nontraditional family while the rest of the class observes and records feedback. Class discussion follows.

B. Objectives:
You will be able to:
1. Recognize initial goals and treatment phases in working with families.
2. Evaluate a family role play.
3. Formulate suggestions for effective treatment.

C. Procedure:

1. Before beginning the exercise, review the material in the text on beginnings with families. It emphasizes information which will be the focus of the exercise.[1] Initial goals include:
   a. Get a clear picture of the problem.
   b. Gain the family's consent to treatment.
   c. Set procedures for change in motion.

   The five phases for beginning treatment include:
   a. Alleviate or at least minimize early apprehension.
   b. Ask family members to explain what's wrong.
   c. Establish agreement about what's wrong.
   d. Concentrate on how family members relate to each other.
   e. Establish commitment to a plan of action.

2. Read the role-play described below. Volunteers are needed for each role. Otherwise, your instructor will assign roles.

Role Play: A Nontraditional Family

Social Work Role:
The social workers are counselors at a family services clinic. They accept call-in referrals and provide short-term counseling, emphasizing problem solving, primarily to families. On occasion, they provide individual counseling to family members in order to work on specific issues or problems.

The Situation:
This is the first interview with June Cleaver, her daughter, Waleeta, sixteen, and son, Beaver, eleven. June and her ex-husband Ward have just completed the divorce process. June called the agency in panic because of pain and confusion resulting from the divorce. You received the information presented below from the intake worker's report.

Client Role:
June, thirty-eight, is a mild-mannered, friendly, responsive, attractive woman who is overwhelmed and confused by her recent divorce. After graduating from high school, she worked three years as a secretary and married Ward. Since her marriage, she has not worked outside the home. She has been involved in many civic organizations such as the Ladies Aid.

(continued)

[1] The initial goals and five phases presented here are primarily based on material found in *Family Treatment in Social Work Practice* by C. Janzen and O. Harris (Itasca, IL: F.E. Peacock, 1986).

June thought everything in the marriage was fine—granted, a bit dull, but fine. She and Ward had a nice house and raised two fine children. People had often commented on what a fine relationship they had. They virtually never fought with each other. As a matter of fact, things were so comfortable between them that they rarely even talked with each other anymore.

Suddenly Ward broke the news to her that he had met another woman. He told June that he loved this woman and wanted to marry her. Six months later, June found herself divorced.

Ward, forty-two, is a relatively well-to-do small businessman who owns and runs a small Pacman outlet store. He fell in love with Barbie, twenty-six, his attractive secretary. Ward told June that he has much more in common with Barbie than he ever had with June. He told June that he loved his children and respected her, but could no longer stay in the marriage.

June is especially concerned about her present financial status. The divorce agreement mandated that she and Ward sell their home and divide the equity. This amounted to only $7,500 for each. Her total current income is $695 per month from child support. She questions whether she can do anything other than housework. She has little confidence in her own abilities.

She always thought she would grow old with Ward, living in a nice, secure, middle-class home. Now she feels her world has been shattered.

Client Role:
Waleeta is a pleasant yet assertive young woman. She has many friends and has always been a loving, well-behaved child.

Waleeta is angry and disappointed with her parents. She feels they've been keeping a big secret from her. She's angry at her father for running off with another woman and angry at her mother for letting him.

She especially has difficulties when she visits her father on weekends. She resents her new stepmother, Barbie, and has frequent arguments with her.

Although Waleeta has always been a B+ student in school, her grades have been slipping recently. She can't seem to concentrate anymore. She's worried about her parents, her lack of money for clothes and activities, herself, and relationships in general. She feels that the world has let her down.

Client Role:
Beaver is really Theodore, but everybody calls him the Beaver because he's so cute. Beaver has always been a happy, active (although a bit feisty) child. He's been well-behaved, although he has had a tendency to get into minor trouble like accidentally breaking windows or losing report cards on the way home from school. Although many of his friends have tried smoking Camels and drinking Rot-a-gut apple wine, Beaver always felt this was bad and avoided "going along with the crowd."

His father's leaving really confused him. He doesn't know quite what to do. He feels frightened and insecure. He feels more tempted now to do some of the "bad" things his friends do.

3. The role players should position themselves where the rest of the class can observe them clearly.
4. The role play should last no longer than twenty-five minutes. Your instructor will tell you when it should stop. The workers should focus on the goals and phases cited above. The clients should do their best to play the roles assigned.
5. Observers should note their reactions during the role play on the role play feedback form.

Role Play Feedback Form

a. What do you think are particularly *good techniques* used by the social workers? How did the *clients react* to these techniques? (Please be specific.)

b. Do you see any weaknesses or areas in which improvement would be helpful? (Specific suggestions for how to improve are beneficial.)

c. Do you have any additional thoughts or comments?

6. After the role play is finished, your instructor will lead a class discussion for approximately fifteen minutes focusing on the following questions:
   a. What feedback did you note on your forms?
   b. What were the strengths of the role play?

c. What were some of the critical points during the role play?
d. What techniques did the workers use that were exceptionally helpful?
e. What weaknesses were evident in the role play?
f. What suggestions do you have for improvement? Please be specific.
g. How did the workers feel about how the role play progressed?
h. How did the clients feel at the critical points of the role play?
i. To what extent did the workers achieve their initial goals?

Exercise 2: A Lesbian Parent Coming Out

A. Brief description:
Volunteers role play a worker and a gay parent who is struggling with telling her children she's a lesbian while the rest of the class observes and records feedback. Class discussion follows.

B. Objectives:
You will be able to:
1. Recognize some of the issues involved when lesbian or gay people come out to their children.
2. Evaluate the effectiveness of a role play addressing the issue of coming out.
3. Propose suggestions for dealing with this issue.

C. Procedure:
1. Before beginning this exercise, review the material in the text on gay/lesbian families.
2. Read the role play described below. Volunteers are needed for each role player. Otherwise, your instructor will assign roles.

Role Play: A Lesbian Parent Coming Out

Social Work Role:
The worker is a social worker at Happy Hoppy Tots, a large day care center. Her role is to address family adjustment problems involving the center's children, provide consultation regarding children's behavior to the center's "teachers," and help parents get the resources they need.

The worker has been working with Frieda for the past six months. Frieda, thirty-one, is the mother of Angelo, four, a client at the center. The problem involved Angelo's temper tantrums. Specifically, the worker helped Frieda apply behavior modification techniques at home (for example, time-outs) and

(continued)

coordinated Angelo's behavior management with his teachers at the center. Improving control at home is related to improved control at the center. Angelo's behavior has significantly improved. The worker and Frieda have developed a good rapport.

Client Role:
Frieda is a quiet, inconspicuous woman who works as a claims adjuster for an insurance company. Frieda also has another son, Harry, eight, living with her at home. She divorced Angelo and Harry's father six years ago.

Frieda is grateful to the social worker for helping her with Angelo's temper tantrums. She is not usually one to talk about herself a lot or share her feelings. However, she has come to trust the worker and to appreciate the worker's competence.

The Situation:
Frieda approaches the worker one day during one of their meetings. The two have been meeting regularly to discuss Angelo's progress.

Suddenly, Frieda blurts out to the worker, "I can't stand hiding anymore. I'm a lesbian. How can I tell my children? Can you help me?"

3. The role players should position themselves where the rest of the class can observe them clearly.
4. The role play should last no longer than twenty-five minutes. Your instructor will tell you when it should stop. The worker should focus on helping Frieda decide what to do about coming out to her children. The person playing Frieda should feel free to make up and elaborate things about her role play life.
5. Observers should note their reactions during the role play on the role play feedback form.

Role Play Feedback Form

a. What do you think are particularly *good techniques* used by the social workers? How did the *clients react* to these techniques? (Please be specific.)

(continued)

b. Do you see any weaknesses or areas in which improvement would be helpful? (Specific suggestions for how to improve are beneficial.)

c. Do you have any additional thoughts or comments?

6. After the role play is finished, your instructor will lead a class discussion for approximately fifteen minutes focusing on the following questions:
   a. What feedback did you note on your forms?
   b. What were the strengths of the role play?
   c. What were some of the critical points during the role play?
   d. What techniques did the workers use that were exceptionally helpful?
   e. What weaknesses were evident in the role play?
   f. What suggestions do you have for improvement? Please be specific.
   g. How did the worker feel about how the role play progressed?
   h. How did Frieda feel at the critical points of the role play?
   i. To what extent did the worker help Frieda make a decision about telling her children that she is a lesbian?

Exercise 3: Working with Multiproblem Families

A. Brief description:
Volunteers role play workers and members of a multiproblem family, while the rest of the class observes and records feedback. Class discussion follows.

B. Objectives:
You will be able to:
1. Recognize some of the issues involved in multiproblem families.
2. Evaluate the effectiveness of a role play focusing on such a family.
3. Propose suggestions for effective interventions.

C. Procedure:

1. Before beginning this exercise, review chapter 10 in the text, especially the material on multiproblem families. Primary suggestions include:
   a. Don't get overwhelmed yourself.
   b. Follow the problem solving process as you would in any other practice situation.
   c. Partialize and prioritize problems.
   d. Determine which, if any, problems you can work on yourself.
   e. Identify and use relevant community resources.
2. Read the role play described below. Volunteers are needed for each role player. Otherwise, your instructor will assign roles.

Role Play: Multiproblem Families

Social Work Role:
The social workers are part of the family services unit in a large public welfare department in an urban county. The workers' job includes assessing the family's problems and needs, making referrals to community resources, and providing some short-term family counseling when necessary.

The Situation:
This is the third meeting with a six-person family that has come to the department because it is plagued with a multitude of problems and doesn't know where else to turn. Individual characters and problems are described below. This information was gathered during the two prior meetings when all family members were present. The workers are now at the point of establishing a plan of action.

Client Roles:

Ozzie, forty, spouse and father, is partially disabled in his legs because of a car accident. He can only walk for short distances and stand for short periods of time. He says he's depressed, feels useless, is unhappy, and has become quite "crabby." He describes himself normally as being rather quiet and reserved.

Ozzie is a high school graduate who had worked as a clerk in the city garbage collection department's office for nineteen years. He got laid off twenty-seven months ago due to departmental budget cuts. At that time, his annual salary had been $24,000.

Ozzie feels detached from his family and out of control. He has never been very involved with the children as he felt that was mostly Harriet's job.

Ozzie has defined the family's problems as follows (in unprioritized order):

- General lack of money.
- Inability to pay the rent or buy food.
- The leg is "acting up" and he needs medical attention for it, but has neither money nor insurance to pay for it.
- Almost constant fighting with Harriet.

(continued)

- Feelings of inadequacy as a provider and as a husband.
- Recent sexual impotence.
- Not even enough money for booze.
- Annoyance with Grandma Hildegarde.

Harriet, thirty-two, spouse and mother, is a quiet, attractive person who has devoted her life to her family. She has an 11th grade education as she dropped out of high school to marry Ozzie. She does not consider herself to be very bright. In school, she had been placed in special education classes. She now works part-time at the Choosy Chunky Chicken Packing Plant, packing Chunky Chicken for minimum wage. Harriet has some trouble organizing household tasks and planning ahead, so she relies a lot on her mother (Grandma Hildegarde, who lives with the family) to help her make decisions.

Harriet perceives the family's problems as being the following (again in unprioritized order):

- Lack of money.
- Because of inability to pay the rent, the landlord's threatening to evict them.
- Worry over Ozzie's drinking (recently when he gets drunk, he's threatened to hit the kids).
- Fighting with Ozzie.
- Having trouble controlling the kids' behavior.
- Generally being overwhelmed and confused.

Grandma Hildegarde, sixty-nine, lives with the family for financial reasons. She expresses a generally cynical, pessimistic attitude and often dwells on "what a terrible life" she's had. She tends to interfere in Ozzie and Harriet's relationship and likes to tell them both what to do. She does love the children, especially Ricky, and likes to spend time with them. Her favorite pastime is watching daytime soap operas, especially "One Life to Live."

Hildegarde's perceptions of the family's problems include the following:

- Lack of money.
- Her social security check seems to get smaller every month.
- "Life is cruel."

Davida, fifteen, is Ozzie and Harriet's daughter. She is an outgoing, rebellious person to whom sarcasm comes easily. She is doing poorly in school, has flunked one grade, and has a truancy problem. She likes to stay out late with friends, especially older boys who are on probation. She was caught twice snorting coke in school. She is not one who likes to share how she really feels about things, especially her personal life and her family. She frequently fights with her parents.

(continued)

The following are the problems as Davida perceives them:

- Lack of money.
- Frightened of being hit by her father when he's drunk (he's threatened her twice).
- Being sick and tired of fighting with her parents.
- Thinking that she's ugly.
- Wanting to go steady with one of the older guys she hangs out with.
- Being pretty depressed about life.
- Worry that she may be pregnant and not knowing what to do about it (she's not exactly certain who the father is).

Ricky, ten, has a shy, quiet personality. He doesn't have many friends. He maintains a C average in school. He doesn't like to do what his parents tell him to do (for example, going to bed when he's supposed to or doing the dishes). He has a close relationship with Grandma Hildegarde.

Ricky sees the problems as follows:

- Stopping his parents from constantly telling him what to do.
- Stopping his parents from fighting with each other all the time.
- Stopping his father from fighting with Grandma Hildegarde.
- Wanting more money, especially a greater weekly allowance.

Biff, thirteen, exhibits a "tough guy" attitude. He likes to be seen as the strong, mean, lean, killing machine, silent type. He doesn't say much but is usually sarcastic when he does. He's bored that he has to be involved in this interview. He doesn't feel very emotionally involved with the other members of his family except for Davida, over whom he tends to be protective. He spends most of his time with his gang, the Heavy Metals. He attends school irregularly, but has always managed to pass.

David's perception of the family's problems include the following:

- Wanting to "get out of here" and back to the Heavy Metals.
- Wondering how to make money almost any way he can.

3. The role players should position themselves where the rest of the class can observe them clearly.
4. The role play should last no longer than twenty-five minutes. Your instructor will tell you when it should stop. The workers should focus on implementing the suggestions for working with multiproblem families. The clients should portray their respective roles as best they can and elaborate details wherever they feel it's necessary.
5. Observers should note their reactions during the role play on the role play feedback from below.

Role Play Feedback Form

a. What do you think are particularly *good techniques* used by the social workers? How did the *clients react* to these techniques? (Please be specific.)

b. Do you see any weaknesses or areas in which improvement would be helpful? (Specific suggestions for how to improve are beneficial.)

c. Do you have any additional thoughts or comments?

6. After the role play is finished, your instructor will lead a class discussion for approximately fifteen minutes, focusing on the following questions:
   a. What feedback did you note on your forms?
   b. What were the strengths of the role play?
   c. What were some of the critical points during the role play?
   d. What techniques did the workers use that were exceptionally helpful?
   e. What weaknesses were evident in the role play?
   f. What suggestions do you have for improvement? Please be specific.
   g. How did the worker feel about how the role play progressed?
   h. How did the clients feel at the role play's critical points?
   i. What is your impression of multiproblem families?

j. To what extent do you feel that the family portrayed in this role play resembles multiproblem families in real life?
k. To what extent did the workers achieve the goals noted above for working with multiproblem families?

Exercise 4: Practicing Specific Techniques

A. Brief description:
Students are asked to volunteer for a family role play where workers demonstrate the implementation of reframing or role playing. Subsequently, the class evaluates the process.

B. Objectives:
You will be able to:
1. Describe reframing, or role playing.
2. Demonstrate the technique within the context of a family role play.
3. Assess the implementation of the technique.

C. Procedure:
1. Select reframing or role playing and review the related explanatory material provided in the text.
2. Select one of the role plays described in Exercises 1 through 3 above.
3. Volunteers are needed to portray the worker(s) and client(s) involved in the chosen role play. The goal will be to utilize the chosen technique within that role play context.
4. Continue the role play for up to twenty minutes. By that time, the workers should have been able to implement the technique. The instructor may end the role play earlier if the workers finish implementing the technique earlier.
5. With the entire class, discuss for about ten minutes the following questions and issues:
   a. How was the chosen technique implemented in the role play?
   b. What suggestions do you have to improve implementation of the technique?
   c. What did you learn about the technique from observing the role play?
   d. How did the workers feel about implementing the technique?
   e. How did the clients feel about participating as the workers implemented the technique?
   f. How useful do you think this technique might be in real practice situations?

11 Values, Ethics, and the Resolution of Ethical Dilemmas

I. **Introduction**

II. **The NASW *Code of Ethics***

A. Six Core Values:

1. Service
2. Social justice
3. Dignity and worth of the person
4. Importance of human relationships
5. Integrity
6. Competence

B. Six Major Aims:

1. Identifying primary social work values
2. Summarizing broad ethical principles as guidelines for practice
3. Helping determine relevant considerations when addressing an ethical dilemma
4. Providing broad ethical standards for the public in general to which it may hold the profession accountable
5. Socializing new practitioners to the mission, goals, and ethics inherent in the profession
6. Articulating specific standards that the profession may use to judge its members' conduct

C. Ethical Principles: Based on the six core values, set forth standards to which all practitioners should strive

D. Ethical Standards

Highlight 11.1: A Summary of Ethical Standards in the NASW Code of Ethics

1. Social worker's ethical responsibilities to clients
    a. 1.01 Commitment to clients
    b. 1.02 Self-determination
    c. 1.03 Informed consent
    d. 1.04 Competence
    e. 1.05 Cultural competence and social diversity
    f. 1.06 Conflicts of interest
    g. 1.07 Privacy and confidentiality
    h. 1.08 Access to records
    i. 1.09 Sexual relationships
    j. 1.10 Physical contact
    k. 1.11 Sexual harassment
    l. 1.12 Derogatory language
    m. 1.13 Payment for services
    n. 1.14 Clients who lack decision-making capacity
    o. 1.15 Interruption of services
    p. 1.16 Termination of services
2. Social workers' ethical responsibilities to colleagues

a. 2.01 Respect

b. 2.02 Confidentiality

c. 2.03 Interdisciplinary collaboration

d. 2.04 Disputes involving colleagues

e. 2.05 Consultation

f. 2.06 Referral for services

g. 2.07 Sexual relationships

h. 2.08 Sexual harassment

i. 2.09 Impairment of colleagues

j. 2.10 Incompetence of colleagues

k. 2.11 Unethical conduct of colleagues

3. Social workers' ethical responsibilities in practice settings

a. 3.01 Supervision and consultation

b. 3.02 Education and training

c. 3.03 Performance evaluation

d. 3.04 Client records

e. 3.05 Billing

f. 3.06 Client transfer

g. 3.07 Administration

h. 3.08 Continuing education and staff development

i. 3.09 Commitments to employers

j. 3.10 Labor-management disputes

4. Social workers' ethical responsibilities as professionals

a. 4.01 Competence

b. 4.02 Discrimination

c. 4.03 Private conduct

d. 4.04 Dishonesty, fraud, and deception

e. 4.05 Impairment

f. 4.06 Misrepresentation

g. 4.07 Solicitations

h. 4.08 Acknowledging credit

5. Social workers' ethical responsibilities to the social work profession

a. 5.01 Integrity of the profession

b. 5.02 Evaluation and research

6. Social workers' ethical responsibilities to the broader society

a. 6.01 Social welfare

b. 6.02 Public participation

c. 6.03 Public emergencies

d. 6.04 Social and political action

III. The Canadian Association of Social Workers' *Code of Ethics*

Highlight 11.2: The Canadian Association of Social Workers' Code of Ethics: A Summary of Major Principles

A. Ethical duties and obligations

B. Ethical responsibilities

IV. Ethical Dilemmas: Being faced with a situation where a decision must be made under circumstances where two or more ethical principles are in conflict

V. Conceptualizing and Addressing an Ethical Dilemma: Decision-Making Steps

Figure 11.1: Conceptualizing an Ethical Dilemma:

A. Step 1: Recognize the Problem

B. Step 2: Investigate the Variables Involved

C. Step 3: Get Feedback from Others

D. Step 4: Appraise What Values and Ethical Standards Apply to the Dilemma

E. Step 5: Evaluate the Dilemma on the Basis of Established Ethical Principles

F. Step 6: Identify and Think About Possible Alternatives to Pursue

G. Step 7: Weigh the Pros and Cons of Each Alternative

H. Step 8: Make Your Decision

VI. Ranking Ethical Principles: Loewenberg and Dolgoff's "Ethical Principles Screen"

Figure 11.2: A Hierarchy of Ethical Rights: ETHICS for U

A. Principle #1: People Have the Right to *E*xist with Their Basic Needs Met

B. Principle #2: People Have the Right to *T*reatment That Is Fair and Equal

C. Principle #3: People Have the Right to *H*ave Free Choice and Freedom

D. Principle #4: People Have the Right to Experience *I*njury That Is Minimal or Nonexistent

E. Principle #5: People Have the Right to *C*ultivate a Good Quality of Life

F. Principle #6: People Have the Right to *S*ecure Their Privacy and Confidentiality

G. Principle #7: People Have the Right to *U*nderstand the Truth and All Available Information

H. Postscript

VII. Discussion and Resolution of Ethical Dilemmas in Generalist Practice Contexts

A. Confidentiality and Privileged Communication

Highlight 11.3: Confidentiality and Persons Living with AIDS

1. Relative confidentiality

2. Privilege

3. Court decisions and issues

a. *Tarasoff v. The Regents of the University of California* (1996)

b. *Jaffe v. Redmond* (1996)

c. Limitations on confidentiality

B. Self-Determination and Paternalism

1. Self-determination: Recognizes the rights and needs of clients to be free to make their own choices and decisions

2. Paternalism: Action that interferes with the client's wishes or freedom "for his own good"

3. Informed consent: Workers should clearly inform clients about the purposes, risks, limitations, possible costs, alternatives, right of refusal, and time frames concerning the services provided

4. Clients' decision-making capacity: Social workers may limit clients' right to self-determination when, in the social workers' professional judgment, clients' actions or potential actions pose a serious, foreseeable, and imminent risk to themselves or others. Also, to act on behalf of clients who lack the capacity to make informed decisions

5. Examples

C. Telling the Truth

1. Examples

D. Laws, Policies, and Regulations

1. Examples

E. Whistle-Blowing: Informing those people in positions of influence or authority outside an organization about the existence of an organization's practices that are illegal, wasteful, dangerous, or otherwise contrary to its stated policies

1. Questions to consider before blowing the whistle:

a. How great is the threat to the potential victims?

b. How solid is your evidence?

c. Are there less severe alternative measures to remedy the problem?

d. Can you assume the burden of risk?

2. Recommendations for whistle-blowers

a. Clearly define the variables involved

b. Know your rights

c. Be prepared for the consequences

d. Follow the chain of command

e. Establish a clearly defined plan of action

F. Distribution of Limited Resources

1. Equality

2. Need

3. Client's ability to pay or contribute to his or her community in the future

G. Personal and Professional Values

VIII. Chapter Summary

EXPERIENTIAL EXERCISES AND SIMULATIONS

Four exercises in this chapter cover various aspects of ethical decision making. The first exercise presents an ethical dilemma experienced by a social worker with a B.S.W. degree in a typical human service agency. The second exercise confronts a worker with an ethical challenge arising from the actions of a professional colleague. The client's rights conflict with the professional judgment of the worker in the third exercise. In each of these exercises you will be asked several questions and invited to give your reactions to the situation. In the final exercise, you will be participating in a debate about several naturally occurring ethical dilemmas.

Exercise 1: Mike Howard's Dilemma

A. Brief description:
In this exercise, you will encounter an ethical dilemma faced by a social worker in a human service agency. After discussing the dilemma in a group, you will report your decision to the entire class.

B. Objectives
You will be able to:
1. Recognize ethical dilemmas when they arise in your work with clients or other systems.
2. Use the NASW *Code of Ethics* as a guide for your professional behavior.

C. Procedure:
1. Review the NASW *Code of Ethics* cited and discussed in the text which governs the professional behavior of social workers.
2. The instructor will divide class members into groups of four or six students, with one member identified as the recorder.
3. The instructor will read the case illustration noted below and answer any questions about the activity.

Case Illustration

Mike Howard is a social worker assigned to the family services unit of the Murphy County Department of Human Services. Mike has been working at this agency for about six months. His clients are primarily young mothers who are at risk for child abuse or neglect. Deputy Sheriff Alan Simpson, a friend of Mike's from their days in high school, has contacted Mike about a recent burglary in the county. Alan believes that one of Mike's clients, Jerri Smith, has an item of stolen property in her possession. The item is a twenty-five-inch color televison set which Alan believes was stolen by Jerri's boyfriend and later given to Jerri as a gift. Alan does not believe that Jerri knows the property is stolen. He gives Mike a detailed description of the stolen set and wants Mike to check out Jerri's apartment when he visits her later this week. Mike is asked to let Deputy Simpson know if he spots the stolen set.

4. Within your groups, take about ten minutes to identify the ethical dilemma(s).
5. Refer to the NASW *Code of Ethics* and appraise what professional values apply.
6. Review the hierarchy of ethical principles, ETHICS for U, and determine which levels apply to this situation. Establish a group consensus regarding what you would do in this situation.
7. Report your decision to the entire class.
8. The instructor will lead a class discussion focusing on the following questions:
   a. What made this an ethical dilemma for Mike?

b. What professional values supported by the NASW *Code of Ethics* apply to this case?
c. What principles in the hierarchy of ethical principles, ETHICS for U, apply?
d. What is your duty to your client and to society in this case?
e. Consider Mike's options. How might each of his choices affect his relationship with the client and his friend?
f. To which person is his obligation greater? Why?
g. Should Mike consult his supervisor before making a decision? Why or why not?

Exercise 2: The Case of the Missing Experience

A. Brief description:
A situation is presented where one of your close colleagues has misrepresented her qualifications on an employment form. You are faced with making an ethical decision regarding what to do about it.

B. Objectives:
You will be able to:
1. Use the NASW *Code of Ethics* and the hierarchy of ethical principles, ETHICS for U, to help resolve an ethical dilemma.
2. Make an ethically correct decision about a difficult situation.

C. Procedure:
1. Review the NASW *Code of Ethics* and ETHICS for U as guides for helping you make ethical decisions.
2. The instructor will review the case situation described below for the entire class.
3. In the space provided, write down your answers to each of the questions listed below the case description. Take about ten minutes.
4. Your instructor will lead a class discussion about each of the questions. Be prepared to share your answers with the rest of the class.

Case Situation

Gemma Howser is a social worker with the Piedmont City Health Department. She is primarily responsible for doing HIV counseling with clients who have tested positive, and case management with those receiving longer-term care. Her agency is in the process of expanding services and will be hiring a new social worker. Gemma's supervisor asks her to look at the job applications as they arrive.

As Gemma reviews the job applications and resumés received for the position, she notices one from a colleague from another agency in the community. Gemma has known Zena Carson for many years and is very familiar with her education and background. What is surprising is that Zena says in her application

(continued)

that she has a minimum of two thousand hours in clinical work with clients, one of the job requirements for this new position. However, Gemma knows that this is not the case since none of Zena's positions since graduation has involved this type of clinical work. Moreover, a review of her resumé does not show any evidence of this experience. Gemma is troubled. She considers the following options:

1. Call Zena and ask her about the obviously inaccurate job application.
2. Tell her supervisor that Zena does not have the required two thousand hours and quietly have them pass over her application.
3. File a complaint with the NASW Commission on Inquiry stating that an NASW member has misrepresented her qualifications.

Questions to be considered:

1. What professional values cited in the NASW *Code of Ethics* apply to this case?

2. What ethical principles in the hierarchy ETHICS for U apply here?

3. Are there other options which Gemma should consider?

4. What are the advantages and disadvantages of each of these options?

(continued)

5. What are the most important issues at stake in this scenario?

6. If you were Gemma, what would you do and why?

Exercise 3: The Client's Choice

A. Brief description:
This exercise highlights conflict between client and worker over the best intervention for an identified problem. As the worker, your recommendation is based upon sound research and the most up-to-date information available. The client's decision is based upon questionable judgment and inaccurate information. As in the other exercises, your opinion of what should be done will need to be guided by the *Code of Ethics* and the ethical principles screen ETHICS for U.

B. Objectives:
You will be able to:
1. Recognize the potential conflicts which can occur between a social worker's professional knowledge and the client's rights.
2. Make a decision in cases which involve these two competing issues.

C. Procedure:
1. The instructor will divide you into groups of six to seven people. Select one person in each group to serve as the recorder.
2. Review the case situation presented below. By yourself, without group input, answer the questions listed after the case situation.
3. Discuss the case situation within your group and come to a consensus on the best answers to each of the questions.
4. The instructor will ask each group to report its answers to the larger class.

Case Situation

Judy Allison has a severe eating disorder, known as bulimia nervosa, which can be life threatening. This condition is one "in which a pathologically excessive appetite with episodic eating binges is sometimes following by purging. The purging may occur through such means as self-induced vomiting, or the abuse of laxatives, diet pills, or diuretics. Bulimia usually starts as a means of dieting."[1] She was admitted to the hospital two days ago after her sister found her unconscious in the bathroom of the home they share. As a hospital social worker, you have interviewed Judy at the request of the physician who has been treating her during her hospital stay.

Judy acknowledges she has a serious problem, but says a friend told her that it can be cured by a diet of fruits and vegetables. You are unaware of any current research for treating this illness that involves the diet she describes. Instead, you are aware of two treatment programs which have been very successful in treating this disorder. Both are multidisciplinary programs offering inpatient and outpatient treatment, individual and group therapy, and follow-up. You recommend that Judy consider entering one of these programs and offer to have a representative of the program contact her. Judy says she'd rather try the new diet her friend told her about first. She refuses further treatment.

Questions to be considered:

1. If you are the worker, what is your obligation, if any, to encourage and convince Judy to pursue effective treatment?

2. What professional values and ethical principles conflict in this situation?

(continued)

[1] R. Barker, *The Social Work Dictionary* (Silver Spring, MD: The National Association of Social Workers, 1995) p. 43.

3. At what point (if any) does a professional have an obligation or duty to ignore the client's expressed choice?

4. If you determined (after proper consultation) that Judy's new diet could be life-threatening, what would you do?

Exercise 4: What Is the Ethical Thing to Do?

A. Brief description:
Students are divided into small groups. Each group is presented with an ethical dilemma. They discuss the case and come to a decision about what to do, after which the group shares findings with the entire class.

B. Objectives:
You will be able to:
1. Examine a range of ethical dilemmas occurring in practice.
2. Propose resolutions and identify the professional values and ethical principles upon which that resolution is based.

C. Procedure:
1. Review the material on ethical standards proposed by the NASW *Code of Ethics* and on the hierarchy of ethical principles ETHICS for U.
2. The instructor will divide the class into groups of four or five students. Each group will be assigned one of the ethical dilemmas identified below. Students will be allowed approximately fifteen minutes to discuss the dilemma, evaluate professional values and ethical principles, and come to a decision about what to do.[2]

---

[2] Instructors should note that these exercises may be addressed in a variety of ways depending on class size. Students may individually be assigned a dilemma to address and subsequently present their findings to the class. Groups may be assigned more than one dilemma. Dilemmas may be read out loud to the class, after which students may participate in a large group discussion.

ACCESS TO RECORDS

Breech of Confidentiality

Tell her yes He did file a complaint but you will investigate each side for the best interest of the child.

Ethical Dilemma #1

Yvonne is a child protective services worker. After receiving a referral, she or other assigned workers will "investigate reports of child abuse and neglect, assess the degree of harm and the ongoing risk of harm to the child, determine whether the child can remain safely in the home or should be placed in the custody of the state, and work closely with the family or juvenile court regarding appropriate plans for the child's safety and well-being"(Liederman, 1995, p. 425).

Yvonne has a client, Lolita, four, who was allegedly abused by both parents. Lolita currently resides with her mother, Reza, while Reza is receiving counseling and other services including job training. Bill, Lolita's father, no longer lives in the home but has told Yvonne he would like to seek custody of Lolita. Bill calls Yvonne to complain about Reza's treatment of Lolita. He states that Lolita often wets her bed at night and Reza simply ignores it. Reza subsequently allows Lolita to sleep in her wet bed. Then, even worse, the next day or night Reza does not change the sheets for Lolita. Yvonne notes carefully what Bill tells her in Lolita's case record.

The next day, Reza calls Yvonne in a panic. She cries that Bill is threatening to take Lolita away from her. Reza says Bill told her he called Yvonne to complain about Reza's treatment of Lolita. Reza stresses that she does not want to lose her little girl. She demands to see Yvonne's records.

What should Yvonne do: show Reza the incriminating records, or not?

Ethical Dilemma #2

Herman is a substance abuse counselor. He is currently seeing an alcoholic client, Anne, age thirty-seven. Herman views Anne as a timid, needy woman who is working on increasing her self-esteem, problem solving skills, and assertiveness in the context of addressing her alcoholism problem. Treatment is going exceptionally well. Anne has not been drinking for months and has been attending Alcoholics Anonymous meetings regularly. Anne is very grateful to Herman for all she feels he has done for her. One day at the end of the counseling session, Anne walks up to Herman and says, "I really need a hug!" What should Herman do? On the one hand, Anne is needy of approval and affection. She wishes to convey her gratitude to Herman. On the other, he does not want to convey inappropriate feelings that do not exist.

Should he allow her to hug him or not?

Ethical Dilemma #3

Sue married Jim two years after the biological father of her daughter Andrea disappeared seemingly from the face of the earth. They have now been married for seven years. Andrea, eight, and Jim have become very close. Jim feels just like Andrea is his biological daughter. Jim and Sue pursue the possibility of Jim adopting Andrea. Mary Ellen is the adoptions worker assigned to the case. She helps with the relatively complex process of having the biological father relinquish his parental rights for Andrea when he is nowhere to be found. Mary Ellen has completed a number of stepparent adoptions and has become quite competent in their successful completion. Jim and Sue are very thankful. They give Mary Ellen a $50 gift certificate for a popular local restaurant.

Is this appropriate or not? Should Mary Ellen keep the gift or return it? What is the ethical and tactful thing to do?

Ethical Dilemma #4

Lloyd is a social worker at a group home for people who are cognitively challenged or have cognitive disabilities (the former, more negative term is mentally retarded).[3] Ellie, thirty-five, has been a resident at the group home for eight years. She has relatively high adaptive functioning in terms of daily living skills, can read at the fourth grade level, and has successfully worked at a sheltered workshop since entering the group home. She has no known relatives. The court has designated a lawyer as her guardian *ad litem* (that is, a court appointee whose responsibility is to "preserve and manage the affairs of another person who is considered incapable of managing his or her own affairs," especially when court actions are involved) (Barker, 1995, p. 158).

Without warning, Ellie cheerfully approaches Lloyd one day and informs him that she has saved enough money to go to Disney World, her dream of a lifetime. She chatters on about getting the tickets and taking her first airplane ride. Lloyd is familiar with Ellie's capabilities and strongly feels this endeavor is far beyond her capabilities.

What should he do?

[3] *Cognitively challenged* is an alternative term referring to mental retardation. *Mental retardation* is "significantly below-average intellectual functioning and potential, with onset before age 18, resulting in limitation in communication, self-care and self-direction, home living, social and interpersonal skills, use of community resources, academic skills, work, leisure, health, and safety" (Barker, 1995, p. 232). Many professionals feel that referring to such individuals as being cognitively challenged is far more positive than using the term mentally retarded (DeWeaver, 1995).

Ethical Dilemma #5

Ricardo is a social services worker who specializes in teaching parents effective child management skills. Over the past six months, he has been working with Irma, a former crack user, to gain control of her four children's behavior. Although it was very difficult at first for Irma to trust Ricardo, they now have established a trusting relationship in which Irma feels free to discuss difficult issues with Ricardo. Ideally, Ricardo would like to continue work with Irma for the next several months. However, he has been transferred to another unit's position with a higher salary. Irma has achieved many of the major goals, but still could make significant improvements in how she treats her children. Ricardo feels it would be very difficult for Irma to become accustomed to and work with another worker.

What should he do?

Ethical Dilemma #6

Nick is a counselor for teenagers with severe emotional and behavioral problems who reside in a residential treatment center. He sees himself as a shy person who finds it difficult to confront issues in conflictual situations. As a member of an interdisciplinary team, he attends a staffing for one of his clients at which progress is reviewed and future plans established. Dr. Schmaltz, the psychiatrist attending the meeting, is a powerful, authoritarian man who makes strong points completely in opposition to what Nick is proposing for the client being reviewed. Dr. Schmaltz commands much authority and respect among other staff.

What should Nick do?

Ethical Dilemma #7

Chuck is a youth counselor at an urban YMCA.[4] He is in his early twenties, good at sports, familiar with young people's jargon, and, thus, extremely popular with his teenage clientele. Emilio is another youth counselor at the same agency. One night after work, Emilio accidentally observes Chuck smoking a joint with two of his clients in the shadows of an alley. After serious thought, the next day Emilio confronts Chuck about his behavior. Chuck responds that it was only marijuana and it provided a way for him to "join with" and be accepted by some of his clients. Chuck rationalizes that smoking joints prevents many young people from using harder, more dangerous drugs. Chuck implies that Emilio is just jealous of Chuck's good rapport with the clientele.

What should Emilio do now?

---

[4] *YMCA* refers to the Young Men's Christian Association. They are a "worldwide group of organizations devoted to the physical, intellectual, social, and spiritual well-being of young men" (Barker, 1995, p. 413). One should note that they no longer restrict themselves to Christians.

Ethical Dilemma #8

Willie Lee, twenty-three, is a resident in a center for people who have cognitive disabilities. Willie Lee can eat by himself and take care of most of his daily hygiene needs. His vocabulary is small, but he usually understands much more than he can express. Willie Lee is a very friendly person who socializes well with peers and is generally respectful of staff. He looks forward to his father's rare visits, sometimes only once or twice a year. His mother died at his birth.

Willie Lee's father, Horace, has recently remarried and is moving across the continent. He has hired an attorney and wants to terminate his guardianship and responsibility for Willie Lee. Horace has always found Willie Lee a burden and been embarrassed by his disability. Horace feels this is his chance to abandon the whole problem and not think about it anymore. Although Willie Lee is always happy when Horace visits, he never asks about him. This may be partially due to Willie Lee's communication difficulties.

Horace succeeds in terminating his rights and moves away. He informs the center that he plans on having no further contact with Willie Lee.

Should the center social worker inform Willie Lee of this turn of events? Does Willie Lee have the right to know about his father's status?

Ethical Dilemma #9

Ling, eighty-six, is a bed-bound resident in a nursing home. Although she has numerous physical difficulties, she has maintained fairly strong mental faculties. She enjoys the company of her two daughters who visit regularly. Ling's physician has just discovered that Ling has developed a lethal form of intestinal cancer and has only weeks, possibly a few months, to live. Ling's daughters beg the nursing home social worker not to tell Ling of her condition. They plan to visit Ling daily and want her to enjoy her time as best she can. They feel that informing her about the cancer would only ruin her last days.

What should the social worker do? Should she inform Ling of her condition? What are the pros and cons of informing or not informing?

Ethical Dilemma #10

Sissy is a financial assistance worker. Agency policy requires her to report any extra income clients may earn. The exact amount of such income is then deducted from their financial assistance checks. An excited client, Bertha, with four children, burst out, "I'm so happy! My neighbor is going to pay me to take care of her two children while she works. This will do wonders for my grocery bill."

As her worker, what should Sissy do? Should she report the additional income and thereby decrease her financial assistance check? If so, should she tell Bertha what she plans to do? What might Bertha's reaction be? Or should Sissy keep her statement confidential, thereby disobeying agency policy? What is the ethical thing to do?

Ethical Dilemma #11

Chuck works for a social services agency serving almost all Hispanic and African American clients. All the social workers and administrators are white. None of the professional staff speak Spanish.[5] Chuck is very concerned about this situation, but hesitates to make waves. It is such a major problem. He feels too insignificant to take it on himself. Yet, he can't keep it from bothering him.

How might clients be better served? What are the agency's needs? What options might Chuck consider pursuing? What is the ethical thing to do?

Ethical Dilemma #12

Lai is a social worker at a shelter and treatment center for runaways. The center typically uses volunteers to serve many of its functions, including counseling youth and families. Although volunteers receive twenty hours of training, Lai feel this does not make them competent to counsel young people and their families.

What, if anything, is wrong with this agency's volunteer policy? What might Lai do to make changes? What might those changes be? What is the ethical thing to do?

3. After approximately fifteen minutes, the instructor will call the groups back to join the entire class. Representatives from each group will first read the vignette depicting their assigned dilemma, and then describe their decision about what to do.
4. The entire class then discusses the group's decision and debates its merit. Alternative solutions may be proposed.

---

[5] This vignette is adapted from one presented in B. Cournoyer, *The Social Work Skills Workbook*, 2nd ed. (Pacific Grove, CA: Brooks/Cole, 1996) p. 72.

12 Ethnically and Racially Sensitive Social Work Practice

I. Introduction

II. Diversity in the United States

A. Terminology

Highlight 12.1: Common Terminology

1. Ethnocentrism: An orientation or set of beliefs that holds that one's own culture, racial, or ethnic group or nation is inherently superior to others
2. Individual racism: The negative attitudes one person has about all members of a racial or ethnic group
3. Institutional racism: Those policies, practices, or procedures embedded in bureaucratic structures that systematically lead to unequal outcomes for people of color
4. Minority: One term for a group, or a member of a group, of people of a distinct racial, religious, ethnic, or political identity that is smaller or less powerful than the community's controlling group
5. People of color: People whose skin color differs from that of the community's predominant group

B. Historic and Current Discrimination

III. Barriers to Effective Multicultural Social Work

A. Continued Acceptance of the Myth of the Melting Pot

B. Assumption that All Who Come to Our Country Will Be Overjoyed to Be Here

C. Tendency to Explain a Person's Behavior by Reference to Her Culture

D. An Attempt to Be Color-Blind

E. Tendency to Assume that Words Mean the Same Thing to Everyone

F. Assumption that Clients Think as You Do

G. Expectation that Clients Will Understand the Social Worker's Role

H. Insufficient Self-Awareness

I. Absence of a Repertoire of Effective, Multicultural Intervention Techniques

J. Lack of Knowledge of the Culture and Experiences of Specific Groups with Whom You Are Likely to Work

IV. Integrating Ethnic and Racial Sensitivity in the Generalist Intervention Model

A. Engagement

1. Approach clients from multicultural groups with a clear understanding of their own view of the world and how it differs from that of others

    a. Individuals who have routinely experienced discrimination and oppression may approach the process with trepidation, anger, or distrust

    b. Recent immigrants may not be familiar with American norms

c. Stigma associated with mental health problems may be a barrier

d. Platicando: Informal and leisurely chatting that contributes to the warm atmosphere

e. Eye-contact interpretation

B. Assessment

1. Client is operating in dual environments: the dominant one and the one associated with their ethnic or racial background

2. Recognize the client system strengths

3. Recognize that different approaches to understanding and treating physical or emotional illness reflect group traditions

4. Be aware of your own way of thinking about a client's situation

5. Concern of client's cultural and racial identity

6. Responsiveness of agencies to the needs of multicultural groups

C. Planning

1. Confront community social problems that can be influenced by differences among multicultural groups

2. Possibly consider the family as the client instead of the individual when working with Asian or African American clients

3. Possibly include the elderly in Hispanic and Asian families in the planning process

D. Implementation

1. Short stories or analogies may be more effective in approaching a topic with Hispanic and Asian clients to alleviate feeling threatened
2. Nonverbal communication may have greater importance than spoken words
3. Workers may need to self-disclose more than usual

E. Evaluation

1. Recognize that much of the research reported in literature has limited generalizability
2. Involve the client directly in the evaluation process
3. Consider whether or not the method needs to be adapted to multicultural groups
4. Instruments that were normed on Anglo Americans cannot be used with equal validity on other groups

F. Termination and Follow-Up

1. Take time to discuss diversity issues that were dealt with in prior stages
2. If termination occurs prematurely, offer client the opportunity to come back at any time

V. Practical Knowledge and Skills

A. Native Americans

1. Understand the unique differences

a. Resided here first

b. Range from highly sophisticated social system to more simple organization

c. Massive efforts to teach "white man's ways" have deprived many children from learning the traditional child-rearing approaches

d. Child abuse was relatively unknown until recently because corporal punishment was rare

e. Many of the poor parenting skills today can be traced to boarding school treatment of parents

f. Traditional cultural styles are significantly different from most European cultures

2. The value of time: Native Americans do not share the near obsession with time that white Americans have (less rigid with appointment times)

3. Native American noninterference

    a. Need time to get to know worker

    b. Participatory, self-directed relationships have greater value

    c. Silence and lack of peer pressure are common

    d. Group decisions are more likely to take precedence over individual decisions

4. Communication patterns

    a. More nonverbal

    b. Not a loud culture

c. Deference to authority and individual dignity

d. Do not self-disclose readily

e. Family loyalty important

f. Less likely to brag

g. Praise in front of others may be embarrassing

5. Fatalism: May hold attitude that events are fixed in advance for all time in such a manner that human beings are powerless to change them

6. Sharing is more important than acquiring

7. Attending skills

    a. Leaning forward may be seen as intruding into the life space of another

    b. Sustained eye contact is considered rude

8. Intervention styles

    a. Restatement, clarification, summarization, reflection, and empathy can be useful

    b. Client-centered strategies are less likely to work

    c. Network therapy may be helpful

    d. Involvement in other aspects of the client's life may increase trust

9. A cautionary note

    a. Histories and tribal experiences are quite often different

    b. Consider a continuum of lifestyles

1) Traditional

2) Marginal

3) Middle-class

4) Pan-Indian

a) Multitribe perspective

b) Less likely to use Anglo health services or mental health organizations

B. Hispanics

1. General information

a. One of the fastest-growing multicultural groups in the United States

b. Covers a wide group of nations

2. Family centering

a. "Family" may be both nuclear and extended relatives as well as friends and neighbors

b. Father is primary authority figure

c. Children owe respect and debt to their parents

d. Individualism must occur within the context of the family and traditional Hispanic values

e. Efforts to increase independence of individual family members may be culturally inappropriate

3. Parental roles

a. Father less likely to express emotional support

b. May appear aloof, expects to be obeyed

c. Expected to earn a living

d. Mother's role is typically to balance father's

e. Encouraging family involvement is often wise

4. Communication patterns

a. Strong nonverbal tradition

b. Interviews should reflect informality

5. Fatalism

a. Plays major role in outlook on the future

b. Future-oriented approaches less important than service offered right now

6. Bilingualism

a. Shortage of bilingual workers will stymie efforts to serve large groups of Hispanics

b. Children having to learn two languages may be a source of stress for them

7. Intervention styles

a. A more directive approach

b. Use fewer reflective techniques

8. A cautionary note: Never assume a client is controlled by cultural, ethnic, or racial experience

C. African Americans

1. General information

a. Only group who came here as slaves

b. Continuous history of maltreatment

c. Have substantially lower per-capita income, despite level of education

d. Almost 30 percent of families live in poverty

2. Communication patterns

a. Ebonics

b. Do not try to adopt a language you are not comfortable with

c. If you don't understand, ask for clarification

d. May be reluctant to reveal personal weakness

e. Be aware how past interactions with social systems have reinforced or extinguished certain behaviors

3. Family experiences

a. Religion plays important role

b. Extended family play important role

c. Include extended family in decision making

4. Intervention styles

a. Show respect by using their formal names and titles; do not use nicknames, and so on, unless invited to do so

b. Study African American literature, music, and newspapers

c. Brokering is very effective

d. Avoid vague possibilities

e. Empowerment should be emphasized

f. Afrocentricity

1) Rationality and emotionality are equally important

2) Concern with objectivity is inconsistent with Afrocentricity

g. Assess if race or ethnicity is a factor within the institutional or organizational environment

5. Macro-level approaches to intervention

6. A cautionary note

D. Asian American and Pacific Islanders

1. General information

a. Asians and Pacific Islanders are not homogeneous

b. Between-group differences

c. Within-group differences

Highlight 12.2: Within-Group Differences

1) Migrational experiences

2) Location of residence

3) Degree of assimilation/acculturation

4) Degree of fluency with one's native language

5) Degree of fluency with English

6) Extent of identification with one's country or region of origin

7) Level and location of education

8) Age

9) Composition and degree of intactness of one's family

10) Level of integration into formal and informal networks

11) Religious/spiritual beliefs and values

12) Financial resources

13) Whether both parents are from the same nation

d. Filial piety: Devotion to and compliance with parental and familial authority

e. May have sense of guilt or shame in seeking social services

f. "Losing face"

2. Family centering

a. Clients reluctant to discuss problems with nonfamily members

b. Father is head of family—whenever possible, work through father when planning interventions

c. Recent and older immigrants may request specific services: advocacy and brokering

d. American-born Asians are more likely to accept counseling and interpersonal interventions

e. Refugees will be different from other immigrants

f. Less likely to show feeling

3. Communication patterns

   a. More nonverbal than verbal

   b. Nodding may simply mean understanding, not agreement

   c. Learn their names (which is family name, and which is given name)

4. Attending skills

   a. Avoidance of eye contact typical

   b. In some cultures, it is an insult for an adult male to shake the hand of an adult female

   c. newly arrived immigrants are more likely to observe traditional customs

5. Intervention skills

   a. Direct, goal-oriented approach is preferable

   b. Reliability and dependability are virtues

   c. Paraphrasing should seldom be used

   d. Questioning should be used sparingly

   e. View time as elastic, not static

   f. Community-based services are more likely to be accepted and used

   g. Group-oriented, rather than self-oriented

   h. Cognitive approaches are more useful

   i. Recognize the values of indigenous healing approaches

   j. Adopt empowerment approaches accordingly

k. Children should never be used as translators

6. A cautionary note

VI. Developing Effective Cross-Cultural Interventions

A. Cultural Competence

Highlight 12.3: Strategies for Cultural Competence

1. Consider clients first as individuals
2. Do not assume that ethnic identity tells you anything about a person's values or behavior
3. Treat "facts" you have learned about cultural values and traits as hypotheses, and subject them to testing with each new client
4. Remember that multicultural groups are at least bicultural
5. Allow clients to tell you which portions of their cultural history, values, and lifestyle are relevant to your work with them
6. Identify strengths in the client's cultural orientation that you can build upon
7. Be aware of your own attitude about cultural pluralism
8. Engage your client actively in the process of learning what cultural content should be considered by asking clearly about the client's experiences, beliefs, and values
9. Keep in mind that there are no substitutes for good clinical skills, empathy, caring, and a sense of humor
10. Demonstrate interest in a client's traditions and customs
11. Consult traditional healers and spiritual leaders

12. Respect and courtesy are always culturally appropriate

B. Summary

Figure 12.1: A Brief Summary of Cross-Cultural Differences

VII. Chapter Summary

EXPERIENTIAL EXERCISES AND SIMULATIONS

The exercises in this chapter are designed to help students expand their awareness of and sensitivity to cultural differences. The first exercise is essentially a library research project for individual students combined with a classroom activity. The second asks students to look at their own ethnic heritage and how it has influenced their lives. The third exercise asks students to apply their knowledge of cultural differences and deal with their own values as they make decisions in a series of case situations. Finally, the last exercise offers students out-of-class activities which can be combined with in-class discussion, if desired.

Exercise 1: Ethnic Sensitive Strategies

A. Brief description:
Using social work literature, you will locate one source which describes an ethnically and/or racially sensitive intervention strategy and report on this approach in class.

B. Objectives:
You will be able to:
1. List and describe at least one ethnically and/or racially sensitive approach to working with culturally diverse people.
2. Use social work literature to identify techniques and strategies supported by research.

C. Procedure:
1. Locate one journal article, book, or professional paper which describes some aspect of social work practice with people of color. You might begin by looking at the bibliography for your text. In addition, you might wish to consult the *International Index to the Social Sciences, Social Work Research, and Abstracts*, or any computerized database available in your library.
2. Read the article and identify one technique or strategy which the author(s) suggest will be helpful in working with people of color.
3. Prepare a brief (one page) written summary of the technique and a critique of the author's research. In your review, answer these questions:
    a. Describe the approach suggested by the author(s).

b. Does the author cite any research or study which supports his or her suggestions?
c. Does the author mention the work of any other writers in her or his material?
d. With which group(s) would this approach be most successful, according to the author(s)?
e. Would you be comfortable using this approach? Why or why not?

4. Briefly report on your findings in class. Be prepared to answer any questions from the instructor or other students.
5. Turn your one-page paper in at the end of the class.

Exercise 2: Ethnic Heritage

A. Brief description:
Using your life experiences, you will begin to recognize the ways in which your life and behavior have been influenced by ethnic heritage.

B. Objectives:
You will be able to:
1. Identify several ways in which your life has been influenced by your cultural and ethnic heritage.
2. Understand the importance of ethnic heritage in shaping behavior, beliefs, and perceptions.

C. Procedure:
1. List the ethnic groups with which you most identify. This might include German, Polish, Nigerian, Japanese, etc.
2. Identify the country(ies) from which your grandparents or great-grandparents came.
3. Record any religious orientation held by your great-grandparents, grandparents, parents, and you.
4. Look at the list you have produced. Which groups (ethnic, cultural, religious, and so on) have affected your development? Think about the messages which you have received from each of these groups. What are the behaviors, attitudes, beliefs, and values transmitted by these groups? To what extent are you in agreement with these? Which have you rejected and why? What advantages or benefits have you experienced because of your background? What disadvantages, if any, have you experienced?
5. In what ways might your own cultural heritage affect your work as a social worker? Is being aware of your heritage likely to enhance or detract from your ability to work with people from different groups? Why?
6. The instructor will go around the class asking each member to identify his or her primary ethnic groups, one behavior, belief, value, or attitude which he or she carries forward from this heritage, and one which has been rejected or not accepted. She or he will then lead a general discussion around the questions posed in procedure 5 above.

Exercise 3: Tough Decisions

A. Brief description:
You will be presented with several brief case situations and asked to discuss the actions you would take in each. You will complete this exercise in a group.

B. Objectives:
You will be able to:
1. Recognize a series of typical situations involving people of color and consider various strategies for handling each.
2. Develop sensitivity to unanticipated consequences of initially positive activities.

C. Procedure:
1. The instructor will divide the class into groups of four to six students. Each group will be asked to read the case situation and decide how to answer the questions which follow. A group may have a majority answer and a minority answer if it cannot come to consensus on a particular question.

Case Situation #1

Mary Wong and Mary Perez have both applied for the Social Worker I position in your agency. Both have similar educational backgrounds, and neither has experience since they just graduated from the same B.S.W. program. Mary Wong, who is Chinese, and Mary Perez, who is Mexican-American, are both qualified for the position. If you were in a position to hire one of them, what further information would you need or like to have? If both are equally qualified, upon what would you base your decision?

Case Situation #2

Assume that Mary Wong is not Chinese, but is married to Richard Wong, who is. Does this change your decision-making process in any way? Why or why not?

Case Situation #3

Roberto and Ernesto Rivas have been picked up by the police for shoplifting. You are the social worker responsible for doing an initial assessment and either recommending information (non-court) intervention or referring them to juvenile court for a finding of delinquency. What information would you need before making a decision? Does the ethnic or cultural background of the clients make any difference in what you might do? Why or why not?

Case Situation #4

You are a school social worker. The teacher has referred to you a young Native American boy who she says is "too quiet" in class. According to the teacher, he speaks only when spoken to and rarely makes eye contact with her. She is concerned that he is having a problem relating to her and is afraid that his quietness will cause him academic problems eventually. What will you say to the teacher? To the boy? Why?

Exercise 3: Understanding Culturally Sanctioned Behavior

A. Brief description:
You will be given three case situations involving behavior deemed inappropriate or problematic by others. Your task will be to identify which aspects of the behavior appear to be culturally sanctioned (approved).

B. Objectives:
You will be able to:
1. Recognize culturally sanctioned behavior.
2. Suggest strategies for working with people from different cultures.

C. Procedure:
1. On your own, read each case situation below and answer the questions.

Case Situation #1

Alice is a twenty-seven-year-old Native American woman who lives with her two children. She is unmarried and currently lives on welfare. She works a part-time job, but the combination of welfare and the job still leaves her strapped for money. Her nineteen-year-old sister moved in with Alice about a month ago, though she has no income, no job, and few employment-related skills. Alice is now helping to support her sister as well as her own children. However, when asked about this, Alice sees nothing wrong with the arrangement and can't understand why anyone would find it odd.

a. Is Alice's behavior culturally sanctioned?

b. Why do you think this behavior is culturally sanctioned? Why not?

(continued)

c. If you were Alice's social worker, what would you do in this situation and why?

Case Situation #2

Juanita Villa is seventeen years old and a senior in high school. She mentions to her teacher that she must get home right after school and cannot attend the school dance. She explains that her father does not want her spending time with young men and that she is not yet able to date. Juanita is not really complaining, but the teacher senses that she would really like to attend the dance. The teacher mentions this case to you over lunch and asks your opinion.

a. Is Juanita's father behaving in a culturally sanctioned manner?

b. Why do you think this behavior is culturally sanctioned? Why not?

c. What would you suggest to the teacher and why?

Case Situation #3

Roseanna, fifteen, is the daughter of a Chinese-American family, all of whom are college educated. She tells her friends that she is not interested in going to college but that her parents expect her to. She feels enormous pressure to do well in high school and to get into a good college. Some of her friends encourage her to talk with the school social worker, which is how you came to know Roseanna.

a. Is Roseanna's family behaving in a culturally sanctioned manner by expecting her to do well in school and to go to college?

b. Why do you think this behavior is culturally sanctioned? Why not?

c. As the school social worker, what, if anything, would you do?

2. The instructor will begin a discussion by asking for volunteers to give their answers to each of these cases. Once each case has been reviewed and several students have shared their opinions, the following questions will be open for discussion:
   a. When a behavior is culturally sanctioned, when might a social worker choose to intervene?
   b. When culturally sanctioned behaviors clash with values of the larger society, which have precedence? Why?
   c. When cultural and larger society values conflict, what values of the social work profession come into play?
   d. Are there any attending skills which might be especially important in working with the individuals and families described in the above cases?

Exercise 4: Out-of-Class Experiences

A. Brief description:
A series of exercises and activities is presented for use outside of the classroom. By your involvement in these activities, you will be exposed to various experiences not replicable in the classroom.

B. Objectives:
You will be able to:
1. Recognize common experiences of people from different cultures.
2. Develop increased understanding of human behavior as it is shaped by cultural experiences.

C. Procedure:
1. Select one of the following activities and follow the instructions.

Activity #1

Make a visit to an ethnic neighborhood in your community or in a nearby city. Participate in one or more activities within that community. Examples include:

a. Attend a church service.
b. Shop at rummage or garage sales.
c. Eat lunch or dinner in an ethnic restaurant.
d. Purchase food in a neighborhood grocery.
e. Attend an after-school sporting event or play.

Keep a log of what you learn. Each log should contain a description of what you did, what thoughts you had about the experience, what your feelings were, and what you learned about the ethnic group or culture which you observed.

Activity #2

Develop a set of questions about the ethnic experiences of members of a particular people of color, e.g., African Americans. You might wish to ask about any discrimination they have experienced while attending your college or university. Similarly, you might ask what values were most stressed by their families or what messages they received about the value of education. Type these questions on a single sheet of paper. Prepare two copies of this questionnaire.

Interview two students of color on your campus. Explain that the assignment is part of a learning activity for a social work course. Write down your interviewee's answers on your questionnaire.

Summarize your findings in a short (two- to three-page) paper. In the paper explain why you selected certain questions and indicate the answers you received to those questions. Do the answers on the questionnaire diverge from what you know about the cultural group being interviewed? What might explain the divergence?

Activity #3

Attend a Native American powwow or other ethnic celebration and participate in as many activities as possible. Observe both verbal and nonverbal behavior of other participants. Note these in a notebook along with your immediate reaction to the behavior.

Later, review you observations. Classify those that appear to be consistent with your knowledge of a particular culture and those which are equally common in the general society. Were there some behaviors which you could not classify? If so, list those. Look at your reactions which you recorded at the time the behavior occurred. In retrospect, do any of them appear to be culturally insensitive or biased by the viewpoint of your own culture (ethnocentric)?

2. Turn your paper or log in to your instructor.

13 Gender Sensitive Social Work Practice

I. Introduction

II. Gender Sensitivity

A. Sexism: Prejudice or discrimination based on sex

B. Sex (or Gender) Role Stereotypes: Expectations about how people should behave based upon their gender

C. Oppression: The social act of placing severe restrictions on a group or institution

D. Sex Discrimination: Treating people differently based on their sex

E. Facts:

1. Women who work full-time earn 74.6 percent of what men earn full-time
2. Nearly 59 percent of all women work outside of the home
3. Women are clustered in low-paying supportive occupations, while men tend to assume higher-paying occupations
4. Women earn significantly less than men in the same job category doing the same work
5. Women are twice as likely as men to be poor within their lifetimes
6. Slightly over one-third of all female-headed households are poor
7. Facts about rape:

   a. Every six minutes a woman reports being raped

b. Of every ten rapes, only one is reported

c. Twenty-five percent of women are raped sometime in their lives

III. Women and the Generalist Intervention Model

A. Engagement

B. Assessment

C. Planning

D. Implementation

E. Evaluation

F. Termination

G. Follow-Up

IV. A Feminist Perspective on Micro, Mezzo, and Macro Aspects of Generalist Practice

Highlight 13.1: Are You a Feminist?

Highlight 13.2: Principles of Feminist Counseling

A. Feminist Counseling

1. A client's problems should be viewed "within a sociopolitical framework"

2. Clients need encouragement to free themselves from traditional gender role bonds

3. Intervention should focus on the identification and enhancement of clients' strengths rather than on pathologies

4. Women should be encouraged to develop "an independent identity that is not defined by one's relationships with others"
5. Other women are considered valuable and important
6. Feminist intervention emphasizes finding a balance between work and personal relationships
7. Whenever possible, the personal power between practitioner and client approaches equality

C. A Definition of Feminism for Practitioners

1. Equality
2. Attitudes and actions
3. All aspects of life
4. Education and advocacy
5. Individual differences

V. Micro Practice with Women: Common Problems

A. Stressful Life Events

1. Personal issues
    a. Powerlessness
    b. Limited behavioral and emotional options
    c. Anger
    d. Inadequate communication skills
    e. Failure to nurture self
    f. Balancing independence with interdependence
    g. Lack of trust in self-direction

h. Old rules and expectations

B. Helping Women in Micro Practice

1. Empowering women

2. Enhancing self-esteem

   a. Help client explore how she feels about herself

   b. Give client feedback about her responses

   c. Help client look more realistically at areas where she is experiencing guilt

   d. Help client accept that most aspects of her life have both positive and negative sides

   e. Help client target areas in which she wants to see improvements

3. Increasing assertiveness

4. The meaning of assertiveness

   a. Nonassertive—Martyr

   b. Aggressive—Persecutor

   c. Assertive—Balancer

   d. Assertiveness training

Highlight 13.3: Each of Us Has Certain Assertive Rights

   a. The right to express your ideas and opinions openly and honestly

   b. The right to be wrong

   c. The right to direct and govern your own life

d. The right to stand up for yourself without unwarranted anxiety and to make choices that are good for you

e. The right *not* to be liked by everyone

f. The right to ask for information if you need it

g. The right to decide not to exercise your assertive rights

5. Other positive approaches for women clients

a. Expanding options

b. Changing rules and expectations

VI. Common Circumstances Facing Women

Highlight 13.4: A Feminist Approach to Macro Practice

1. Values the process of how things are accomplished as much as the final result of the process

2. Adopts a "win-win" rather than a "win-lose" philosophy

3. Emphasizes the importance of interpersonal relationships

4. Places a high value on human diversity

5. Emphasizes the value of employee input

VII. Women as Survivors of Sexual Assault

A. The Feminist Perspective on Sexual Assault: Survivor, not Victim

B. Reactions to Rape

1. Rape trauma syndrome

a. The acute phase

1) Fear

2) Self-blame

b. The long-term reorganization phase

C. Counseling Survivors of Sexual Assaults

1. Emotional issues

a. Provide warmth and support

b. Elicit support from others

c. Rebuild survivor's trust in herself, her environment, and other personal relationships

2. Reporting to the police

3. Medical status of the survivor

D. Macro Perspectives on Sexual Assault

1. General societal responses

2. Current services

VIII. Battered Women

A. A Profile of Battered Women

B. Survivors Versus Victims: A Strengths Perspective

C. The Abusive Perpetrator

D. The Battering Cycle

1. Buildup of stress and tension

2. Explosion

3. Making up

E. Why Does She Stay?

1. Economic dependence

2. Lack of self-confidence

3. Lack of power

4. Fear of the abuser

5. Adherence to traditional beliefs

6. Guilt

7. Fear of isolation

8. Fear for her children

9. Love

F. Counseling Battered Women

1. The police and battered women

2. Shelters for battered women

3. Counseling strategies

    a. Offer support

    b. Emphasize strengths

        1) Believe the client

        2) Discover what the client wants

        3) Move the assessment towards personal and environmental strengths

    c. Review alternatives

    d. Furnish information

    e. A training manual for counselors

        1) The initial interview

        2) Emotional reactions

        3) Specific counseling techniques

G. Suggestions for Macro Practice on Behalf of Battered Women

1. Strengthen legal and criminal justice systems

2. Advocate for establishment of services within community

IX. The Feminization of Poverty

A. Facts About Poverty

Highlight 13.5: Women of Color Are "Doubly Disadvantaged"

1. Families maintained by women comprise 13.7 percent of all white families, 45.9 percent of all African American families, and 23.9 percent of all Hispanic families

2. Over half of persons living in families maintained by black and Hispanic women are poor, compared with 31.8 percent of persons in families maintained by white women

3. Of all families maintained by women, with children under eighteen, 45.7 percent of white families live below the poverty line, compared to 63.2 percent for African American and 68.3 percent for Hispanic families

4. Unemployment rates for white men and women are 5.7 percent and 5.8 percent respectively; for African American men and women, 12.9 and 12.3 percent; and for Hispanic men and women, 9.4 and 11 percent

5. The median incomes for families headed by women are $20,867 for white families, $12,537 for African American families, and $12,603 for Hispanic families

6. Both African American and Hispanic families have experienced a drop in income relative to white families, while experiencing a large increase in female heads-of-household

Highlight 13.6: Women's Salaries in Social Work

B. Micro and Mezzo Perspectives on Women and Poverty

C. Macro Perspectives on Women and Poverty

1. Reforming society's perspective
2. Improving conditions in the workplace
    a. Multiple roles
        1) Possible employer assistance
            a) Provide child care
            b) Offer flexible working hours
            c) Provide better part-time work
            d) Provide adequate mandatory parental child-care leaves at full or partial salary
    b. Jobs are segregated by gender
    c. Lack of positive female role models
    d. Salary discrimination
        1) Work interruption—having children, caring for aging parents
        2) Occupational discrimination by sex
    e. Discrimination in benefits and job loss
    f. Sexual harassment

Highlight 13.7: Confronting Sexual Harassment

1) Confront your harasser

2) Be assertive

3) Document your situation

4) Talk to other people about the problem

5) Get witnesses

3. Improving legislation for equality

a. Antidiscrimination legislation

b. Affirmative action

c. Comparable worth

X. Chapter Summary

EXPERIENTIAL EXERCISES AND SIMULATIONS[1]

Five exercises focus on gender-sensitive social work practice. Exercise 1 concerns the exploration of personal values about a range of gender-related issues. Exercise 2 incorporates a macro perspective on micro practice situations by addressing the distribution of scarce resources. Building on the second exercise, Exercise 3 concerns establishing intervention strategies on behalf of women in need. Exercise 4 addresses the issue of sexual harassment. Finally, Exercise 5 concludes with a values-oriented questionnaire regarding feminism. The exercises are designed to urge students to evaluate their personal values, biases, and opinions regarding the impacts of gender-related oppression. They then aim to help students establish relationships between values (both personal and professional) and actual practice.

---

[1] Exercises 1 through 4 are published with permission of *Arete*, University of South Carolina, College of Social Work, Columbia, SC 29208. The exercises are variations of those published in "Feminist Values and Social Work: A Model for Educating Non-Feminists," by Karen K. Kirst-Ashman, in *Arete*,17 (Summer 1992), pp. 13-25.

Exercise 1: Gender Relations Quiz

A. Brief description:
You will be given a variety of provocative statements concerning male and female gender roles and asked to discuss your own opinions.

B. Objectives:
You will be able to:
1. Recognize your own personal opinions and biases on a number of gender issues which focus on work, leadership, pregnancy, and personal relationships.
2. Examine the distribution of power and opportunity between genders on these issues and assess the extent to which the situations are fair.
3. Formulate suggestions for addressing these issues.
4. Begin to recognize your attempts to deny that attitudinal problems do exist.

C. Procedure:
1. Complete the "Gender Relations Quiz" below. For each statement, check whether you agree or disagree. You must commit yourself to one answer or the other. Additionally, note briefly the reasons for your answers.

Gender Relations Quiz

a. Employers should treat men and women equally in work settings.
☐ Agree ☐ Disagree
Reason: ______________________________
____

b. Men make better supervisors than women.
☐ Agree ☐ Disagree
Reason: ______________________________
____

c. Men make better leaders than women.
☐ Agree ☐ Disagree
Reason: ______________________________
____

d. A woman would probably not be elected president.
☐ Agree ☐ Disagree
Reason: ______________________________
____

(continued)

e. Mothers of small children should remain at home to care for them.

☐ Agree ☐ Disagree

Reason: ______________________________

____

f. Women should automatically be granted several months leave of absence from paid employment when having a baby.

☐ Agree ☐ Disagree

Reason: ______________________________

____

g. Employers should continue paying such women full salary during their absences.

☐ Agree ☐ Disagree

Reason: ______________________________

____

h. In a heterosexual couple, a man should be the "head of the house."

☐ Agree ☐ Disagree

Reason: ______________________________

____

i. Among heterosexual couples, men generally are the "heads of the house."

☐ Agree ☐ Disagree

Reason: ______________________________

____

j. Women and men living together should share housework (for example, taking out the garbage, cleaning the bathroom, doing the laundry, washing dishes, cooking, grocery shopping, taking care of the children) equally.

☐ Agree ☐ Disagree

Reason: ______________________________

____

k. Women and men living together really do share housework equally.

☐ Agree ☐ Disagree

Reason: ______________________________

____

l. If you marry (or are married), you will share (or do share) housework equally with your spouse.

☐ Agree ☐ Disagree

Reason: ______________________________

____

2. Divide into groups of four to six persons. Discuss the Gender Quiz statements, your respective answers, and your rationales for each. After your discussion, a volunteer from each group will be asked to summarize the group's findings and ideas for the entire class.
3. After approximately twenty minutes, each group's volunteer should present her or his summary. Then address with the entire class the following questions:
    a. Is power and opportunity distributed equally between genders? Why or why not?
    b. What are your own opinions and biases about these issues?
    c. How do these coincide with professional social work values?
    d. In those instances where you perceive inequities, what suggestions do you have to make changes?
    e. What can you *personally* do to bring about positive change?

Exercise 2: Allocation of Scarce Resources

A. Brief description:
In small groups you will be directed to allocate a significantly inadequate amount of resources among a variety of women needing services.

B. Objectives:
You will be able to:
1. Recognize the critical significance of scarce resources.
2. Identify some of the gender-related social and legal aspects of oppression.
3. Begin to negotiate a troublesome reality.
4. Evaluate the potential success of such negotiation.

C. Procedure:
1. Divide into small groups of four to six persons.
2. Each group will theoretically have a total of $25,000 that it may allocate to any one of the client situations described below. You may only allocate the total amount to address one situation. Assume that any lesser (or divided) amount would be inadequate to meet the need and, therefore, would be useless.

Situation 1

Julia, age twenty-three, and her four young children are homeless. All the shelters are filled. She married at age seventeen and never worked outside of the home. She and her children had always been poor, her husband jumping from one low-paying, blue-collar job to another. Last month her husband told her he was sick of her and all of his responsibility. He abruptly left without telling her where he was going. Julia has no money at all. She also desperately needs food and clothing for her family. She has no access to relatives or other personal support systems who could help her. Additionally, to remove herself from her homeless situation permanently, she needs job training along with concurrent daycare.

Situation 2

Jeannette, age twenty-nine, was raped fourteen months ago and now has discovered she has AIDS. Her assailant has been apprehended and she has learned he is HIV-positive. Thus, she thinks he was the one who contaminated her. Her health has deteriorated rapidly. She desperately needs expensive health care including the new "cocktail drugs" which could help her keep at least some of the more severe diseases at bay. She had been a secretary. Her health problems no longer allow her to work. Nor does she have any health insurance. Her savings are completely depleted.

Situation 3

Danielle, age fifteen, has been on the streets for two years. She thinks she is cocaine and alcohol addicted. She ran away from home because her stepfather had been sexually abusing her since she was eleven. She couldn't stand it anymore. She needs both a home and an expensive rehabilitation program to survive.

Situation 4

Gertie, age thirty-seven, is a battered wife. The beatings are getting worse and worse. She literally doesn't know how long she can live in her battering environment. She is only one of about 150 battered women identified in the small Midwestern town. Counseling, day care, legal aid, and a place of respite for these women are desperately needed. However, a minimum of $20,000 is required to keep the shelter for them open another three months.

Situation 5

Ruth, age fifty-seven, has been divorced for twenty-three months. Her ex-husband, a businessman two years her senior, left her to run off with a twenty-six-year-old woman. He had an excellent and expensive lawyer. The state in which they lived did not treat divorced women very kindly. Additionally, her ex-husband was able to manipulate most of their assets so that they had become hidden and unavailable to her. She received half of the money from their house and $230 a month in alimony for two years. Their house had been beautiful, but their equity in it had been relatively little. As a result, she now has almost no money left and alimony is about to stop. Her ex-husband has spent thirty-five years establishing a career for himself. He is well off. However, Ruth had spent her life taking care of his home, entertaining his associates, and doing charity work for her community. She has no experience working outside of the home other than the minimum-wage job she has managed to get serving yogurt at a local frozen yogurt store. Her reserve of cash is almost gone. What she earns now will barely pay for her rent, let alone for her food, health care, and other needs. She has no idea about what she will do.

3. Take approximately fifteen minutes for discussion. A volunteer from each group should be prepared to share with the entire class the group's decision regarding how to spend the money.
4. Rejoin the entire class for a discussion which addresses the following questions:
   a. What were your reasons for choosing the situation you did to allocate the resources?
   b. To what extent did you find the experience frustrating and why?
   c. Whose fault was it that each situation occurred?
   d. Did you feel our society failed these people, and, if so, how?
   e. What aspects of policies, social programs, and laws contributed to these people's problems?
   f. Do you see aspects of sexism and oppression based on gender, and, if so, what are they?
   g. How do you think you'd feel if you were in a situation similar to each one described above?

Exercise 3: Proposing Intervention Strategies for Women in Need

A. Brief description:
A series of vignettes illustrating gender-related problems will be presented. You will then be asked to propose alternative intervention strategies for each.

B. Objectives:
You will be able to:
1. Recognize and examine feminist issues more objectively and accurately.
2. Formulate appropriate alternatives for change.
3. Articulate the relationship between feminism and social work.

C. Procedure:
1. Review once more the vignettes presented above in Exercise 2.
2. Break up into small groups of four to six persons.
3. For each vignette, the groups should establish an intervention alternative. Allow thirty minutes for this process.
4. A volunteer from each group should explain the group's recommendation to the entire class. Vignettes should be addressed one at a time. Discussion should focus on which intervention alternatives are most doable and have the greatest potential for effectiveness.
5. Review the definition of feminism. Discuss with the group the extent to which each alternative reflects feminist perspectives.

Exercise 4: Confronting Sexual Harassment

A. Brief description:
You will be asked to respond to a variety of vignettes illustrating incidents of sexual harassment.

B. Objectives:
You will be able to:
1. Define and recognize some aspects of sexual harassment.
2. Explore some of the interpersonal dynamics involved in such incidents.
3. Assess your own feelings and reactions to such treatment.

C. Procedure:
1. Review the material in the text concerning improving conditions in the workplace, especially that about sexual harassment.[2]
2. Read the following vignettes one at a time.

Vignette #1

Ann's boss states that if she doesn't go to bed with him, she won't make it through her six-month probationary period. She really needs the job. She knows she has the right to complain, but knows she would be labeled a troublemaker. The management would probably find a way to "let her go." They had done so with others before. She doesn't know what to do.

Vignette #2

Barbara's male supervisor likes to sneak up behind her and surprise her by putting his arms around her. This makes her feel very uncomfortable. However, he's responsible for scheduling her hours, evaluating her work performance, and giving her salary increases. She is terrified of confronting him.

Vignette #3

Lavinia really needs to get a good grade in a course she's taking with a male professor, Dr. Driven, in order to keep her scholarship and stay in school. So far, she has only achieved a grade of D+. When Lavinia goes to see Dr. Driven, he frequently touches her arm and pats her knee. He acts exceptionally friendly with her. Last Thursday Dr. Driven said he would "see what could be done about improving the grade" if Lavinia would start dating him. Lavinia feels trapped. She doesn't know what to do.

---

[2] There are many additional resources which elaborate upon sexual harassment issues. One excellent source of information is *Sexual Harassment on Campus: A Legal Compendium*, 2nd ed., edited by Elsa Kircher Cole (Washington, D.C.: National Association of College and University Attorneys, 1990).

Vignette #4

One of the other financial assistance workers in the county social services department really annoys *Irene*. The man is constantly telling dirty jokes about women. Additionally, he likes to whistle at any woman under age twenty-five who passes his desk. His favorite phrase in life seems to be, "Wow, look at the big bozooms on that one!"

3. After presenting a vignette, take about ten minutes for each to discuss the following questions:
   a. How does this situation fit the definition of sexual harassment?
   b. To what extent are the victim's feelings valid?
   c. How do you feel about this situation?
   d. What do you think the victim should do?
   e. What do you think you would do in this same situation?

Exercise 5: Are You a Feminist?

A. Brief description:
You will answer a questionnaire regarding feminism and discuss your own values concerning the issue.

B. Objectives:
You will be able to:
1. Explore your feelings about feminism.
2. Identify the definition of feminism.

C. Procedure
1. Review chapter 13, "Gender Sensitive Social Work Practice."
2. Individually, read the questionnaire cited below and check "yes" or "no" for each question.

Questionnaire:
Are You a Feminist?

a. Do you believe that women should have the same rights as men?
☐ Yes ☐ No

b. Do you believe that women should have the same access to jobs and social status as men?
☐ Yes ☐ No

c. Do you believe that women should *not* be discriminated against or *denied* opportunities and choices on the basis of their gender?
☐ Yes ☐ No

d. Do you believe that, ideally, both people's attitudes and behavior should reflect the equal treatment of women?
☐ Yes ☐ No

(continued)

e. Do you think that many people need to become more educated about women's issues?

☐ Yes ☐ No

f. Would you be willing to advocate on behalf of women (for instance, for poor women or women who have been raped)?

☐ Yes ☐ No

g. Do you believe that both men and women have the right to their own individual differences (that is, of course, differences which don't harm other people)?

☐ Yes ☐ No

h. Do you think that our society is generally structured legally, socially, and economically by and for men instead of women? (This last question is probably the most difficult, and, perhaps, the most painful, to answer.)

☐ Yes ☐ No

3. Count the number of times you answered "yes" to the eight questions.
4. Focus specifically on the definition of feminism which includes the following concepts:
    a. Philosophy of equality.
    b. Involvement of both attitudes and actions.
    c. Involvement of all aspects of life.
    d. Necessity of providing education and advocacy.
    e. Appreciation of individual differences.
5. With the entire class, take about fifteen minutes to discuss the following questions and issues:
    a. Are you or are you not a feminist? Explain why or why not.
    b. How would you define feminism?
    c. What negative images does feminism conjure up for many people?
    d. To what extent do feminist principles contradict or coincide with professional social work values?

14 Advocacy

I. **Introduction**

II. **Defining Advocacy**

A. Advocacy and the Generalist Intervention Model

1. Case advocacy: Activity on behalf of a single case

2. Cause advocacy: Addresses an issue of overriding importance to some client group

3. Useful skills in cause advocacy

a. Government documents

b. Political process

c. Public speaking

d. Tolerance for conflict

III. **The Goals of Advocacy**

A. Access to Existing Rights

B. Social Action to Secure New Rights and Entitlements

IV. **Targets of Advocacy**

A. Increase Accessibility of Social Services to Clients

B. Promote Service Delivery that Does Not Detract from Clients' Dignity

C. Assure Equal Access to All Who Are Eligible

Highlight 14.1: Indications for Advocacy

1. When organizational barriers to services are created by agency policies or procedures
2. When clients are refused legally entitled benefits or services
3. When existing services are inadequate
4. When services provided are inhumane or dehumanizing
5. When agencies or staff discriminate against clients
6. When services or benefits are not provided to clients in a manner consistent with the immediacy of their need
7. When multiple clients clearly have the same need for which no services or benefits yet exist
8. When clients cannot adequately protect their own interests or act on their own behalf
9. When existing services or benefits make the situation worse
10. When clients are denied civil rights or other legal protections
11. When clients are denied a voice in the planning for or creation of services
12. When social workers can help clients mobilize in their own interest to obtain services or benefits routinely available to those with more resources
13. When social workers can help achieve social and economic justice for individuals or groups of clients

V. History of Advocacy in Social Work

VI. Assumptions About Advocacy

A. Assumptions About Power

1. Those who hold power are generally reluctant to give it up
2. Those who hold power generally have greater access to resources
3. Resources in general are not distributed equally
4. Conflict is inevitable when those in power treat those with less power unfairly
5. You must have power to change existing organizations and institutions

B. Assumptions About Organizations

1. There are many reasons why organizations and institutions fail to meet client needs
2. Agencies and organizations *do* have potential to change
3. Many agency leaders prefer that workers not advocate for changes in their organization
4. Agencies may subvert the rules or try to be secretive

C. Assumptions About Clients

1. Clients influence and are influenced by their environment
2. Clients should be helped to help themselves
3. Clients should always have prior knowledge and consent of advocacy

VII. Knowledge Required by Advocates

A. Knowing the Rights of Clients

1. Individual

2. Societal—considered more important than individual

B. Avenues of Appeal

1. Entitlements

a. Established by law

b. Based on organizational policy

c. Based on an interpretation of organizational policy

C. Available Resources

1. Attorneys

2. American Civil Liberties Union

3. Legal Aid

4. Alliance for the Mentally Ill

D. Tactics and Strategies of Intervention

1. General intervention skills

2. Skills for particular situations

VIII. Assessment in Advocacy Situations

A. Self-Assessment

B. What Are Your Sources of Power

1. Legitimate power: When person A believes person B has the "right" to influence her

2. Reward power: Ability to provide positive reinforcement to another person
3. Coercive power: Ability of someone to punish or use negative reinforcement on another individual
4. Referent power: One person is influenced by another person because of admiration for that individual
5. Expert power: Those we consider an authority or especially proficient in some area

C. Other Assessment Considerations

1. Nature of the problem
2. Strengths, rights, and resources of the client
3. Characteristics of the adversary

D. The Nature of the Problem Situation

Highlight 14.2: When the System Is Not Working

1. Assessing the client
2. Assessing the adversary
    a. How open to change is the adversary?
    b. What is the degree of vulnerability of the adversary?
    c. How has this adversary handled complaints or challenges in the past?
    d. What are the values of the adversary?

IX. Planning in Advocacy Situations

A. Resources

B. Strategy

C. Tactics

D. The Ultimate Decision

X. Intervention: Advocacy Strategies and Tactics

Highlight 14.3: Guidelines for Advocacy

A. Guidelines

1. Serve only with clear permission of your client
2. Acknowledge that acting as an advocate can impact your relationships with other people and organizations
3. Advocacy is appropriate only to help the client, not to pursue your personal agenda
4. Get the facts first
5. Always enter an advocacy situation with a clear list of concerns and questions
6. Look at issues from both sides
7. Keep a record of things that are said in meetings that relate to your goal
8. Always find out who makes decisions at the next-higher level
9. Record all steps you take to resolve an issue

B. Persuasion

1. Clearly state the issue of concern
2. Allow adequate time for discussion and questions
3. Identify exactly what you want done

4. Summarize areas of agreement
5. Find common ground whenever possible
6. Avoid vague statements
7. Be candid about what you'll do if the problem is not remedied
8. Convey your sincerity and determination to resolve the matter
9. Maintain eye contact and avoid any gestures that might undercut your firmness
10. Approach an adversary as if you both have a desire to resolve things
11. Do not filibuster or monopolize the conversation
12. Do not lose your cool

C. When Persuasion Does Not Work

D. Fair Hearings and Legal Appeals

E. Political and Community Pressure

F. Using the Media

G. Petitioning

XI. Selecting a Strategy for Advocacy

XII. Whistle Blowing

XIII. Legislative Advocacy

Highlight 14.4: Writing Elected Officials

1. Letters to the President
2. Letters to U.S. Senators
3. Letters to members of the House of Representatives

4. Letters to Cabinet Secretaries

A. Factors Affecting Legislative Advocacy

B. Steps in Legislative Advocacy

1. Step 1: Developing and revising the draft bill

2. Step 2: Identifying, obtaining, and maintaining the bill's supporters

3. Step 3: Arranging for sponsorship of the bill

4. Step 4: Introducing the bill

5. Step 5: Working with interest groups to broaden support for the bill

6. Step 6: Educating the public

7. Step 7: Influencing legislative committee consideration

8. Step 8: Influencing action on the floor

IX. Chapter Summary

EXPERIENTIAL EXERCISES AND SIMULATIONS

There are four exercises in this chapter focusing on the topic of advocacy. The first exercise requires the student to assume the role of an advocate in a dispute between tenants and their landlord. The second exercise confronts the worker with a possible whistle-blowing situation which requires careful thought. Exercise 3 provides a flawed example of persuasion and asks the student to identify the mistakes which were made. The last exercise is a letter writing activity based on the premise that social workers will want to (and have to) influence their elected representatives.

Exercise 1: Advocating for Renters

A. Brief description:
You will be deciding appropriate strategies for engaging in advocacy for a specific group of clients. This will give you practice in the role of an advocate.

B. Objectives:
You will be able to:
1. Identify appropriate strategies for advocacy.
2. Determine the logical steps to take to carry out your advocacy.

C. Procedure:
1. The instructor will divide the class into groups of four to six students. Each group will be responsible for reading the case situation and answering the questions. Appoint one person to record each group's decisions.
2. Read the case situation and answer the questions.

Case Situation

The student residents of the Littlejake House were angry. The owner, Dwight Cackle, had taken advantage of Christmas break and began to remodel their apartments without informing them of his intentions. Cackle, hoping to increase his income, was combining an entry hall with portions of the original apartments to create another two apartments. His plan called for shaving three feet off the rooms on either side of the hallway and adding it to the hallway space. The diagram below shows his plan.

The new apartments affect all the residents, who will each lose three feet from the end of their apartments. They will also lose the second exit since all apartments had two exists, one to the hallway and one to the outside. To make matters worse, he has turned off the water in the building since he says he has to do this to work on the new apartments. As a consequence, residents have no water, cannot use the bathrooms, and must listen to the pounding as work on the apartments continues. They have complained to Mr. Cackle, who has told them they're just complainers and he has no intention of stopping work on his project.

As the ombudsman for the student housing office, you have often heard complaints about Mr. Cackle's actions toward tenants, including refusing to return security deposits, not following terms of the lease, and generally abusing residents of his apartments. Now the tenants have come to you for help. You must decide what you can do to assist them.

(continued)

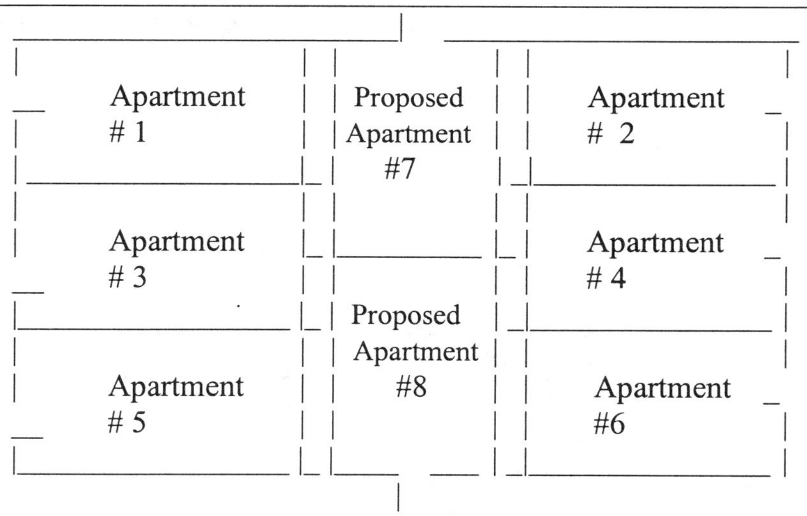

a. Which of the problems appear most serious to you? Why?

b. What information about the tenants would you like to have before attempting to help them?

c. List all possible sources of power available to you and the tenants.

d. What information about Mr. Cackle would help you assess his willingness to respond to your advocacy efforts?

(continued)

e.	What steps would you take to bring about change in this situation?

3. Each group should report its findings to the entire class.

Exercise 2: Whistle Blowing

A. Brief description:
You will confront the situation of an agency worker who learns about unethical behavior on the part of his supervisor.

B. Objectives:
You will be able to:
1. List alternative courses of action.
2. Weight the risks of each course of action.
3. Select a course of action acceptable to you.

C. Procedure:
1. Read the case situation below, placing yourself in the position of Ned. Follow the steps listed after the case situation.

Case Situation

Ned is the chief social worker in a residential treatment center for disturbed adolescent males. He has worked there for eighteen months and likes his job, which consists of planning and leading treatment groups for residents of the center, designing entertainment such as sporting events, dances, and extracurricular activities, and supervising cottage parents who provide day-to-day supervision for the adolescents. In a conversation with a cottage parent, Ned hears an allegation that the treatment center director is pocketing financial donations to the center and diverting other resources to his own use. The cottage parent says this has been going on for a long time and he thought everybody knew about it. You indicate you knew nothing about this.

a. If you were Ned, what would you say to the cottage parent who is your direct subordinate?

(continued)

b. Would you take any steps to determine whether this allegation is true? If so, what steps would you take?

c. If you determined that the allegations were true, what possible steps (if any) might you take?

d. For each possible step, list the advantages and risks involved.

e. Which of the options would you be most likely to pursue? Why?

Exercise 3: Persuasion

A. Brief description:
This case provides an example of a social worker who has not followed the guidelines for persuasion described in the chapter. Your task will be to identify the mistakes made by the worker.

B. Objectives:
You will be able to:
1. Recall the guidelines for persuasion.
2. Identify guidelines which have been misused or otherwise not followed.

C. Procedure:
1. Review the section of the chapter describing the guidelines for persuasion.
2. Read the case illustration and answer the questions.

Case Situation

Naomi Grunge was livid. "You don't care why I'm here or whether my client is in need or not. You have no right!" she shouted at Don Nedlin, Income Maintenance worker for Ashford County Human Services. "My client is entitled to lots of things and you have no basis for denying her," she continued. "What exactly are you asking for?" he said. "I want all my client is entitled to," said Naomi. Don started to respond by reciting the regulations he had to work with. "No! I want none of that crap about regulations. You give my client everything she's supposed to get or else." At that point Don escorted Naomi to the front door of the agency, abruptly turned, and walked back to his office, locking the door behind him as he entered.

a. Which of the eight guidelines on persuading others did Naomi violate?

b. What effect did Naomi's shouting likely have on the person she was trying to persuade?

c. Was the "or else" threat a credible one? Why or why not?

d. Assume that you are a friend of Naomi's and that she would listen to you. What advice would you give her about how to handle this situation?

Exercise 4: Letter Writing

A. Brief description:
Writing letters to elected officials is a common component of the social worker's job. This exercise will give you experience drafting such a letter.

B. Objectives:
You will be able to:
1. Prepare a professional letter having the correct format.
2. Clearly communicate your position on a pending piece of legislation.

C. Procedure:
1. Review the information on writing to elected officials contained in the text.
2. Read the scenario below and draft a letter to Representative Hosea Williamson, your state representative. Give the correct address and salutation and clearly specify your position on the pending legislation. Support your position with several reasons.

Case Situation

You are a member of the Political Action Committee for the state National Association of Social Workers chapter. A bill is pending in your state legislature which will provide funds enabling welfare recipients to receive a college education. Representative Williamson is not yet committed to supporting this bill but may be persuaded if enough of his constituents indicate their interest.

3. Describe three steps you could take (alone, or with the help of colleagues) to convince Representative Williamson.

4. Be prepared to read your letter aloud and to share your steps when the instructor calls upon you.

15 Brokering and Case Management

I. **Introduction**

A. A Definition of Brokering

B. Importance of the Brokering Role in Generalist Practice

II. **The Effective Broker**

A. The Importance of Knowing Resources

1. Eligibility criteria of resource agencies

2. Characteristics of resource agencies

3. Contact persons in resource agencies

B. Types of Resources

1. Community resource directories

Highlight 15.1: Community Resource Directory Index

Highlight 15.2: Resource Directory Listing

2. Telephone books

3. Information and referral services

4. Service organizations and clubs

5. Other information resource systems

C. The Planned Change Process in Brokering

1. Identifying and assessing client needs

2. Identifying and assessing potential resource systems

3. Helping the client select the best resource system

4. Making the referral
5. Helping the client use resource systems
6. Follow-up and evaluation of resource systems

III. Case Management

A. What Is Case Management?

1. Individualization of services
2. Comprehensiveness of services
3. Parsimonious services
4. Fostering autonomy
5. Continuity of care

Highlight 15.3: An Overview of Case Management

a. Definition

b. Purpose

c. Focus

4. Tasks

Figure 15.1: Worker Responsibilities in Case Management

B. Importance of Case Management for Generalist Practice

C. Assessment

1. Assessment of the client's ability to meet environmental challenges
2. Assessment of the caretaking ability of the client's informal support group
3. Assessment of the resources of formal support systems

a. Availability

b. Adequacy

c. Appropriateness

d. Acceptability

e. Accessibility

f. Assessment process:

1) Need-based

2) Holistic/comprehensive

3) Interdisciplinary

4) Participatory

5) A process

6) Systematic

7) A product

Figure 15.2: The Structure of Case Management

D. Planning

1. Service plans

a. Prioritize client needs

b. Establish goals and objectives

c. Identify resource systems involved

d. Identify time frames for delivery of services and achievement of goals

e. Formulate outcome measures

2. Impact goals

3. Service objectives

Figure 15.3: Case Management Plan

Figure 15.4: A Completed Service Plan

E. Implementation

1. Direct services

Highlight 15.4: Motivating Techniques

a. Ask about the plans a client has for himself

b. Contribute realistic suggestions

c. Discuss points of disagreement and work out realistic compromises

d. Develop a contract specifying mutual goals

e. Identify steps that must be taken and the service providers who can help

f. Provide data about service providers

g. Discuss any obstacles the client can foresee in using the proposed services

h. Review responsibilities of each party

2. Indirect services

3. Monitoring

4. Additional roles

F. Evaluation in Case Management

G. Termination in Case Management

H. Follow-Up in Case Management

Highlight 15.5: Case Management for a Client Who Has Mental Disabilities

I. Factors Influencing Case Management Service Delivery

IV. Chapter Summary

EXPERIENTIAL EXERCISES AND SIMULATIONS

The four exercises in this chapter are designed to illustrate the work of the broker and case manager. The first three give experience in thinking about and locating resources, perhaps the most important task of the social worker in the broker role. The last exercise is focused on helping familiarize you with key concepts used in case management.

Exercise 1: Mrs. Darwin

A. Brief Description:
As a task group member in this case, you will be asked to prioritize the problems experienced by the client and identify potential resources which may be accessed.

B. Objectives:
You will be able to:
1. Identify tasks which must be completed in order to assist the client.
2. Prioritize the tasks in order of importance.
3. Identify possible community resources to which the client can be referred.

C. Procedure:
1. The instructor will divide the class into several groups of four to six members. A group recorder will be selected by members of each group.
2. Read the case situation below.

Case Situation

Mr. B. Darwin arrived at the trauma center after suffering a heart attack on the interstate highway. Attempts to revive him failed and the emergency room physician was about to talk to his wife. The Darwins, both in their late sixties, had apparently been traveling through the state on the way to visit relatives.

Mary Ann accompanied the doctor to the trauma center waiting room where they met Mrs. Darwin. A petite woman not even five feet tall, Mrs. Darwin looked very weary. The crumpled handkerchief in her hand was damp from tears. The doctor first introduced herself and Mary Ann. Mary Ann then sat next to Mrs. Darwin.

"Is he dead?" Mrs. Darwin asked quietly. The doctor slowly nodded his head and responded, "Yes, he is."

(continued)

Mrs. Darwin put her head in her hands and cried softly for a minute. She raised her head and asked, "What am I going to do now?"

Mary Ann said that she knew this must be a terrible time for Mrs. Darwin and she offered to do everything she could to help her. She invited Mrs. Darwin to come to the social work office. As the doctor departed, Mary Ann reached out her hand and helped Mrs. Darwin to her feet. Together they took the elevator to Mary Ann's office.

Mary Ann again expressed her sensitivity to Mrs. Darwin's situation and asked her if there was anything that she (Mary Ann) could do. Slowly, Mrs. Darwin described the events of the day that preceded the death of her husband. In a few minutes, Mary Ann discovered the following information.

The Darwins were residents of Wisconsin traveling through Minnesota to visit relatives in Iowa. They had car trouble about fifteen miles from the hospital. When Mr. Darwin got out to check on the car, he fell to the ground. A passing trucker radioed a nearby highway patrol officer, and together they attempted cardiopulmonary resuscitation. Shortly, an ambulance arrived and transported Mr. Darwin to the hospital. The highway patrol officer brought Mrs. Darwin to the hospital with their pet, a small dog. Mrs. Darwin said the car was still on the side of the highway and contained a large load of frozen meat in the trunk. It was to be a gift to her daughter in Iowa, she explained. As they talked, Mary Ann began to make mental notes of the tasks ahead. She also learned a little about Mrs. Darwin. This would prove helpful as they worked together to resolve the woman's concerns.

3. Prepare a list of tasks which must be completed in order to assist this client.
4. Prioritize the tasks from most important to least important.
5. Identify possible community resources to which the client might be referred.
6. A volunteer from each group will be asked to report back to the class on responses to questions 3 through 5.

Exercise 2: Knowing Your Own Resources

A. Brief description:

This activity requires you to assess your own resources. The purpose is to assist you in recognizing the many resources the average person can call upon in times of need.

B. Objectives:

You will be able to:

1. Identify personal resources which might assist you in times of need.
2. Categorize resources according to a predetermined system.

C. Procedure:

1. Read each of the "Need statements" below and list three resources that you could reasonably count on to assist you.

Needs Statements

a. Your car just quit working and you have a doctor's appointment in one hour.
Resource: ____
____
____

b. You are sick and need a prescription picked up at the pharmacy.
Resource: ____
____
____

c. You must pay your tuition of $1,000 by tomorrow morning or your enrollment in classes for this semester will be cancelled.
Resource: ____
____
____

d. You need a pair of dress slacks for a job interview and don't want to have to buy one.
Resource: ____
____
____

e. You need a special book for your social work class tomorrow. The book costs $50. You have only $5 but your part-time job will pay you $75 in one week.
Resource: ____
____
____

f. You have a job interview and need three letters of reference by tomorrow evening.
Resource: ____
____
____

g. You need a haircut or perm by 5:00 p.m. today but have no money.
Resource: ____
____
____

h. You have a date tomorrow night and no transportation. You definitely need a car to drive.
Resource: ____
____
____

(continued)

i. You have a chance for a part-time job that pays rather well, but you need to borrow a rake, hoe, and lawnmower.
Resource: ____
____
____

j. You have nothing to eat in the house and have no money.
Resource: ____
____
____

k. Your computer printer just quit in the middle of your final social work paper, which is due by noon tomorrow.
Resource: ____
____
____

l. You are very sick, don't have a local physician, and don't know what to do.
Resource: ____
____
____

m. Your favorite friend of the opposite sex just broke up with you and you need to talk to someone.
Resource: ____
____
____

Exercise 3: Community Resources

A. Brief description:
In this out-of-class exercise you will be required to identify at least one resource for each of several client needs.

B. Objectives:
You will be able to:
1. Locate resources which might assist clients in meeting specified needs.
2. Learn to use a variety of data sources in your search for client resources.

C. Procedure:
1. Select two of the client situations listed below.

Client Situations

a. Twenty-two-year-old single mother of two children (ages one and three) has just lost her job and has no savings, no family, and no income.
Resource: ______________________________

b. Sixty-eight-year-old man being discharged from hospital to his own home needs a hospital-type bed provided at no charge.
Resource: ______________________________

c. Child has a serious vision disorder and needs corrective surgery. His parents are poor but not on welfare.
Resource: ______________________________

d. Father of six children has just lost his job and needs help locating another.
Resource: ______________________________

e. Homeless family just arrived in town and needs shelter for tonight and tomorrow night.
Resource: ______________________________

f. Child dying of cancer wants to go to Disney World before he dies.
Resource: ______________________________

g. Tenant needs legal advice on whether her landlord can evict her for reporting him to the health department for bug infestation.
Resource: ______________________________

h. Woman battered by her husband needs emergency shelter for herself and her five children.
Resource: ______________________________

i. Alcoholic client needs to know meeting place and time of nearest Alcoholic Anonymous group.
Resource: ______________________________

j. Child burn victim needs reconstructive surgery and parents have no money.
Resource: ______________________________

k. Suicidal client needs to talk with someone immediately.
Resource: ______________________________

2. Using any existing community resource directories, services, or telephone books, locate at least one resource for each of the client situations.
3. List the resource under the problem situation.
4. The instructor will poll the class to determine the resource array which has been located for each problem.

Exercise 4: Matching Concepts

A. Brief description:
A matching exercise using various case management concepts described in the text.

B. Objective:
You will be able to:
1. Correctly match major concepts and their meanings.

C. Procedure:
1. Match the concepts in the left column with the meanings in the right column.
2. The instructor will go through each answer orally after all members of the class are through.

1)	Individuation of services	A.	Person or team who organizes, coordinates, and sustains a network of formal and informal supports and activities to maximize the functioning of people with multiple needs.
2)	Parsimonious services	B.	Discouragement of duplication of service and controlling of costs.
3)	Fostering autonomy	C.	Helping clients become as self-sufficient as possible.
4)	Continuity of care	D.	Developing or designing services specifically to meet client needs.
5)	Comprehensiveness of services	E.	Focus on services meeting client needs in all areas of life including housing, financial, and medical.
6)	Case manager	F.	Assures regular monitoring of clients' needs throughout their lives.

16 Recording in Generalist Social Work Practice

I. **Introduction**

II. **The Importance of Writing in Social Work**

   A. Identifying the Client and the Need

   B. Documenting Services

   C. Maintaining Case Continuity

   D. Interprofessional Communication

   E. Sharing Information with the Client

   F. Facilitating Supervision, Consultation, and Peer Review

   G. Monitoring the Process and Impact of Service

   H. Educate Students and Other Professionals

   I. Providing Data for Administrative Tasks

   J. Providing Data for Research

III. **What Is in the Record?**

   A. Date of Your Interaction

   B. Basic Information about Client

      1. Face Sheet

      Figure 16.1: An Example of a Face Sheet

   C. Reason for Client Contact

   D. More Detailed Information About the Client's Problem and Situation

      1. Intake Form

Figure 16.2: An Example of an Intake Form

2. Social History

Figure 16.3: An Example of a Social History Format

E. Aspects of the Implementation Process

1. Progress notes

Figure 16.4: An Example of a Progress Note Format

F. Follow-Up Information

G. Comments and Questions to Discuss with a Supervisor or Another Worker

IV. Recording Formats

A. Process Recording

Figure 16.5: Portion of a Process Recording with a Client Who Has Just Entered a Nursing Home

B. Using Videotapes and Audiotapes (Get the client's explicit permission)

C. Progress Notes

D. Diagnostic Summary Recording

Highlight 16.1: An Example of a Diagnostic Summary Recording

1. Summary description
2. Presenting problems
3. Peer group relationships
4. Family situation
5. Treatment progress
6. Recommendations
7. Summaries of case conferences

E. Problem-Oriented Recording (POR)

Highlight 16.2: An Amended Case Example of Problem-Oriented Recording

1. Database

2. Problem list

   Figure 16.6: An Example of a Format for Prioritizing Problems

3. Initial Implementation Plans

4. Progress in Plan Implementation (SOAP)

   a. *S*ubjective information

   b. *O*bjective information

   c. *A*ssessments

   d. *P*lans

   Figure 16.7: An Example of a Format for SOAP Progress Notes

F. Advantages of Problem-Oriented Recording

G. Disadvantages of Problem-Oriented Recording

H. Standardized Forms

Figure 16.8: An Example of a Standardized Form

1. Purposes of standardized forms

2. Well-written standardized forms

I. Recording Progress in Groups

Figure 16.9: An Example of a Recording Form for Group Process

J. Writing Letters

Figure 16.10: An Example of a Letter

K. Memos

Figure 16.11: An Example of a Memo

L. Recording in Meetings

1. Agenda

Figure 16.12: An Example of an Agenda

2. Minutes

Figure 16.13: An Example of Minutes for a Meeting

M. Other Types of Recording Formats

V. Technological Advances

A. Computers

Highlight 16.3: Basic Terms in Computer Technology

1. Central Processing Unit (CPU)
2. Memory
3. Hard drive
4. Floppy disk
5. Apple
6. Disk Operating System (DOS)
7. Megabyte
8. Keyboard
9. Monitor
10. Printer
11. Word processing
12. Database software

13. Spreadsheet

14. Management information system

B. E-Mail

C. Faxes

VI. Writing Skills and Recording

Highlight 16.4: Some Basic Good Writing Suggestions

1. Choose your words carefully
2. Avoid slang
3. Avoid words such as always, average, perfect, or all
4. Avoid sexist language
5. Avoid labeling people with terms such as sleazy, strange, punks, slobs, or low class
6. Avoid using abbreviations
7. Be as concise as possible
8. Use paragraphs to divide content into different topics
9. Distinguish between verified facts and your impression of the facts
10. Proofread your written products before they go out

VII. Privacy Principles

A. Confidentiality

B. Abridgment

C. Access

D. Anonymity

Figure 16.14: An Example of a Release of Information Form

VIII. Chapter Summary

EXPERIENTIAL EXERCISES AND SIMULATIONS

Four exercises for this chapter provide different types of writing experiences. They include filling out a standardized face sheet form, recording a social history, writing a memo, and composing a professional letter.

Exercise 1: Filling Out a Face Sheet

A. Brief description:
You will break up into pairs and role-play a client and worker. The worker then interviews the client to get information needed to fill out a form. Class discussion will follow.

B. Objectives:
You will be able to:
1. Recognize the types of information required on a face sheet.
2. Demonstrate how information is gathered to fill out a form.

C. Procedure:
1. Review chapter 16 in the text prior to beginning this exercise.
2. Break up into pairs. Arbitrarily decide who will role-play the worker and who will role-play the client. The worker should interview the client to get the information necessary to fill out the face sheet displayed below. The face sheet is a type of standardized form which provides basic identifying information and is generally placed at the beginning of a client's file. This particular face sheet is for families applying to be foster families. In the role-play, the client should make up answers to the worker's questions.

Foster Home Licensing and Face Sheet[1]

Last Name	Address	Telephone
	City	County

(continued)

[1] This form is adapted from one used by the State of Wisconsin Department of Health and Social Services (DHSS). Printed with permission of the Wisconsin DHSS, 1 West Wilson, Madison, WI.

Husband or Single Person

____
First Name Birthdate

____
Race Religion

____
Occupation

____
Work hours and phone

Ages of own children in home:

Wife

____
First Name Birthdate

____
Race Religion

____
Occupation

____
Work hours and phone

____
Boys

____
Girls

List names and ages of foster children now in home ______________________________

____

Schools foster child might attend ______________________________

____

Special child care skills ______________________________

____

License Information: # of children ______ Sex of children ______
Age of children ______________ Other limitations ______________________
Description of Home: total # of rooms ________ Number of bedrooms ______
Occupants in Home: Number of adults ________ Number of own children ____
Number of other persons (excluding foster children) ______________
Agency responsible for licensing ______________________________
Agency responsible for supervision ______________________________
Date of License: From ____________________ To ________________
Submitted by ______________________________ ________________
Worker Date
Approved by ______________________________

3. After about fifteen minutes, your instructor will end the role play and begin a class discussion focusing on the following questions and issues:
   a. How easy or difficult did the workers find filling out the form?
   b. Were there any areas on the form which you found difficult to fill in? If so, what were they and why were they difficult?
   c. What other types of standardized forms might you have to use in real practice?

Exercise 2: Writing a Social History

A. Brief description:
This is a take-home assignment in which you will be asked to interview a person for information to fill out the social history form provided below.

B. Objectives:
You will be able to:
1. Describe the types of information typically gathered in a social history.
2. Demonstrate how such information is recorded on a standardized social history form.

C. Procedure:
1. Review chapter 16 in the text prior to beginning this exercise.
2. Choose a person you would like to interview. This could be a friend, a relative, or an acquaintance. Explain to the person that social histories reflect the important aspects of an individual's development and help social workers assess the nature of client's problems. Feel free to show the person the social history form. The person needs to know exactly what to expect, especially since you will be asking some personal questions about his or her life.
3. As you interview, fill out the social history form provided below. Remember that the purpose is not to investigate every minute detail of a person's life, but rather to gain a generalized understanding of what's most significant. In a real practice situation, you would be especially attuned to information relating to and clarifying the individual's designated problem. You would also pay special attention to identifying and evaluating the client's strengths.

Social History Format[2]

Name ____________________________ D.O.B. ______________
Address: ____________________________________
Telephone: __________________________________
~~School and Grade:~~ ____________________________
Place of Birth: ______________________________
Religion: ___________________________________

Outline for Social History

I. Family Composition: Draw Genogram
(Note if any parent or sibling is deceased and date)

(continued)

---

[2] Adapted from the form "Outline for Social History." This material is printed with permission of the Community Human Services Department, Waukesha County, 500 Riverview Ave., Waukesha, WI 53188.

<u>Natural Father</u>: <u>D.O.B.</u> ___________
Address:
Occupation:
Religion:

<u>Stepfather:</u> (if appropriate) <u>D.O.B.</u> ___________
Address:
Occupation:
Religion:

Adopted
<u>Natural Mother:</u> <u>D.O.B.</u> ___________
Address:
Occupation:
Religion:

<u>Stepmother:</u> <u>D.O.B.</u> ___________
Address:
Occupation:
Religion:

<u>Siblings:</u>
Name, d.o.b., school, and grade. List all siblings, including those out of home, and current situation. If client or siblings are living with others, state names, addresses, and relationship.

II. <u>Child Under Consideration</u>
Describe personality and physical characteristics.

III. <u>Reason for Referral:</u> Current stressors
Short statement about immediate concern, current situation, and by whom referred. Parent's and child's attitudes about possible placement outside the home.

(continued)

IV. Family Background:

A. Mother:

1. Relationship to each of her parents; relationship between her parents; evidence of emotional disturbance in family.

2. Mother's educational and vocational history.

3. Medical history if pertinent.

4. Previous marriages, with significant details.
Date, Duration
Children born to them

5. History of her courting and marriage, including feelings about marriage and children.

B. Father:

1. Relationship to each of his parents; relationship between his parents; evidence of emotional disturbance in family.

2. Father's educational and vocational history.

3. Medical history if pertinent.

4. Previous marriages, with significant details.

(continued)

5. History of his courting and marriage, including feelings about marriage and children.

C. Family Development:

1. Describe parental relationships, who disciplines whom and how, nature of and reasons for conflicts, family attitude toward current situation, family's financial situation and community involvement, family involvement with law enforcement and mental health agencies. What do you see happening in the family and why? This section should contain a historical perspective and comment on the past as well as the present.

2. <u>Sibling Relationships:</u>
Describe child's relationship with each sibling; to whom child is closest and from whom most alienated; and reaction to birth of next youngest sibling. Describe any specific problems or emotional difficulties siblings in family have or have had in the past and how handled by parents.

3. <u>Other Significant Adults:</u>
Ex-grandparents, aunts, uncles, neighbors, teachers. Indicate who and type of relationship and when it began.

(continued)

4. Environment:
Significance of neighborhoods family has lived in and their dwellings.

V. Personal History of ~~Child~~: Individual

A. ~~Developmental Data~~: Developmental History
Parental relationship during pregnancy, reaction to pregnancy, preferred sex, mother's health (signs of miscarriage, emotional state, significant use or abuse of drugs or alcohol).

N/A

Birth:
Delivery: premature or full term spontaneous? Physical condition of mother and child, length of hospital stay.

N/A N/A

Early Months:
Note any changes in mother's physical or emotional health. Any difficulties in adjusting to the home—was it stable at this time? Did child have colic or other problems? Was child breast or bottle fed? Any feeding difficulties? Note changes in any caretakers and significant losses.

BOTTLE
NO

Later Months and Toddler Stage:
Note ages at which child walked, talked, and was toilet trained. Note any difficulties re: sleep and eating patterns.

W 9 N/A
T 9 N/A
TT 2 1/2 N/A

(continued)

Coordination and Motor Pattern:
A general statement as well as noting any hyperactivity, sluggishness, head or body rocking, random or unorganized activity.

N/A

Parents' feelings regarding above and how they attempted to handle any difficulties.

VERY PLEASED

B. Personality and Social Growth:
Responsiveness: Did child like to be held or did he or she withdraw from people? Did the child play with adults and/or children? Did he or she play in group or prefer to play alone?

YES HELD
BOTH
GROUP

Relationships: Describe relationship with each parent as related by both parents and child. Explore any differences. What about relationships with siblings?

MOTHER = GOOD / NORMAL
FATHER = GOOD / NORMAL
KID STUFF

Separations from either or both parents: When, why, how long? Note also parental and child response toward separating to attend school.

ENGAGED when went to school
only moved to Jackson.

(continued)

Describe child's outstanding traits and fears if any, e.g., is the child happy, sullen, stubborn, dependent, independent? Does she or he have any persistent fears, phobias, or compulsions?

HAPPY Independent

YSO

Discipline: How and by whom? How have parents and child reacted to it?

Mother – Yelled

Sexual development: Amount of sex education. Who provided? Unusual behavior or preoccupations; kind of questions or curiosity displayed; masturbation; parental response.

C. Medical History:

Any illness or disease suffered; injuries, falls, high fevers, convulsions, fainting or other spells, allergies or other somatic disturbances; child and parent reactions. / Also any hospitalization history. Touch on any previous treatment for current problems, previous psychiatric treatment. Type and extent of drug usage, if any. HEART MURMUR = BLUE BABY

TONSILS out

Birth disfigurements, speech defects, enuresis, handicaps.

N/A

Present health.

A OK

(continued)

D. Educational Experiences:

Schools and years attended, achievement, testing dates done by schools, M-Team reports, interpersonal relationships of child; parents' relationship with school systems, extra-curricular activities.

ADRIAN 12YRS.
JCC 1YR
Len. Vo-tech 1YR
BAND, PEP CLUB

Psychological and psychiatric evaluations—previous referrals, contacts, treatment, and progress.

E. Employment Experience:

BUS GIRL / WAITRESS / CASHIER
SECRETARY
F.U.M.C 15 yrs.

VI. Previous Treatment:

Prior placements and services, successful completion or failure of services and/or placements.

Substantiate that care and services that would permit the child to remain at home have been investigated and considered and are not available or likely to become available within a reasonable time to meet the needs of the child.

A. What alternatives to the plan are available?

(continued)

B. What alternatives have been explored?

C. Why are explored alternatives not appropriate?

D. Discuss objectives of rehabilitation, treatment, and care.

VII. <u>Reference Sources:</u>

Label and date interviews, reports, letters used to complete the social history.

Date: ______________________

Prepared by: ______________________
(Social Worker)

Approved by: ______________________
(Supervisor)

SS-153 (Rev. '82)

4. Turn your completed social history in to your instructor for feedback and grading.

Exercise 3: Writing a Memo

A. Brief description:
You will be asked to write a memo concerning a specific issue. You will then break up into pairs and critique each other's work. Class discussion will follow.

B. Objectives:
You will be able to:
1. Recognize the important facets of writing a memo.
2. Compose a memo concerning a specific issue.
3. Evaluate memos.

C. Procedure:
1. Prior to beginning this exercise, review chapter 16, especially the material on memos.
2. In class, read the following situation:

Case Situation

You are a caseworker for Oconomowoc County Social Services. You've been with the agency for a little over a year. All employees are supposed to have an annual performance review. Only workers whose supervisors submit a positive review of the workers' performance will receive a raise in salary for the next year.

You have what you consider an adequate relationship with your supervisor, Chuck Norris. You feel he's neither especially helpful nor knowledgeable. However, he's relatively easy going and lets you do your job "in peace." You get the help and consultation you need from your colleagues and other supervisors in the agency.

The problem is that you've asked Chuck three times, the last in writing, when he has time to sit down with you and do your review. Each time he passed off your request casually and said he didn't have time. The last time you approached him you even subtly reminded him that performance reviews are due within the next week or two. You know that if he doesn't do your review, you won't get a raise next year. You feel you really worked hard this year and really need that raise. Your '90 Dodge Omni is on its last legs and you can't handle the monthly payments for a new car without a raise.

You don't think Chuck really likes to do performance reviews. In fact, you question his overall professional competence. You also don't think he's going to get around to doing your review. You feel that reminding him again would be useless.

You decide that the only way to handle the situation is to contact Chuck's supervisor, Ethyl Metttelschmerz, who is the agency's assistant director. She's very busy with her own responsibilities. You feel the only way to get her attention is to send her a memo about the situation.

You know you must choose your words carefully. You must get your point across without crucifying Chuck. You also don't want to sound angry. You want to state the facts as calmly and nonjudgmentally as possible. You realize that you will have to live with Chuck as your supervisor next year, too.

You write the memo . . .

3. Take fifteen minutes and write a memo to Ethyl about the situation.
4. Your instructor will tell you when the time is up. Break up into pairs and exchange memos. Take about five minutes to write constructive criticisms on your partner's memo.
5. Spend another ten minutes giving each other verbal feedback about the memos. Afterwards, exchange memos again so that you have your own back.
6. Your instructor will call you back to join a full class discussion in which you will address the following questions and issues:
    a. What did you write in your memo?
    b. What was most difficult about writing the memo?
    c. What constructive feedback did your partner give you?
    d. Did you follow the format provided in the text?
    e. What did you learn about writing memos from this exercise?

Exercise 4: Writing Professional Letters

A. Brief description:
You will be asked to write a letter concerning a case situation. Class discussion will follow.

B. Objectives:
You will be able to:
1. Recognize the major components in good letter writing.
2. Compose a letter responding to a case situation.

C. Procedure:
1. Prior to beginning the exercise, review chapter 16, especially the part about writing letters.
2. Read the following:

Case Situation

You are a Case Manager for a local family services agency. A major part of your job is to place young adults with cognitive disabilities in the community and coordinate the supportive services for them.

One of the clients you've recently placed in her own apartment is Holly Wood, twenty-three. She is an attractive, well-dressed young woman who can read at a fifth-grade level. She is proud of her full-time job as a file clerk at a nearby hospital. Although many people with higher intellectual abilities might find this job dull, Holly performs the repetitive tasks involved responsibly and conscientiously. Holly's social life primarily involves a "social club" she belongs to, made up of other developmentally disabled people of similar ability. Group activities are supervised by the family services agency staff.

(continued)

The problem is that Holly's mother, Mrs. DeHavilland, calls you and screams irately that she will not allow Holly to date "those boys" in the social club. She feels strongly that Holly is not able to handle such activities and that she might get involved in "that sex thing."

In fact, Holly has dated two men in the club. One date involve4d a movie and pizza, and the other a baseball game. Although Holly has not as yet gotten serious about any of the men in the club, the potential is certainly there.

Your agency's philosophy is that clients have the right to make their own decisions and to develop relationships just as "normal" people do. Some of the supportive services you coordinate for clients include sex education and counseling to develop responsible decision-making skills. Clients are encouraged and helped to live "normal" lives. They participate in "normal" activities and make "normal" mistakes.

You need to write a letter to Mrs. DeHavilland and tell her in a civil and supportive yet firm way that Holly has the right to make her own decisions. You can stress the help the agency is providing her. You can also emphasize your appreciation for Mrs. DeHavilland's concern about and love for Holly.

3. Using the suggestions for letter writing provided in the text, take fifteen minutes to write the letter mentioned in the vignette above.
4. Your instructor will tell you when it's time to participate in a full class discussion to address the following questions and issues:
   a. What did you write in your letter?
   b. What specific phrases did you choose to get your various points across?
   c. To what extent did you follow the format and suggestions provided in the text?
   d. What did you find most difficult about writing the letter?
   e. What did you learn about letter writing from this experience?